Athlone
—on the Shannon—

Text by Gearoid O'Brien

Paintings by Leila Canney

First published by Cottage Publications,
an imprint of Laurel Cottage Ltd.
Donaghadee, N. Ireland 2008.
Copyrights Reserved.
© Illustrations by Leila Canney 2008.
© Text by Gearoid O'Brien 2008.
All rights reserved.
No part of this book may be reproduced or stored on any media
without the express written permission of the publishers.
Design & origination in Northern Ireland.
Printed & bound in China.
ISBN 978 1 900935 68 5

The Author

Gearoid O'Brien, through an accident of birth, is not quite a native of Athlone. However, he has spent more than nine tenths of his life living here and has spent over thirty years researching the history of Athlone. To make up for his poor credentials he married a true native, the writer and theologian Angela Hanley. They have two adult children, Colman and Carey.

Gearoid attended St. Mary's Infants School, the Dean Kelly Memorial School and St. Aloysius College, Athlone and later studied Librarianship at U.C.D. He is Senior Executive Librarian with Westmeath County Library Service in The Aidan Heavey Library, Athlone and a subject specialist in local studies.

He has written more than a dozen publications on the history of Athlone and Westmeath including *Athlone in old Photographs* (Gill & Macmillan, 2002) he was a co-author with Sean Cahill & Jimmy Casey of *Lough Ree & its Islands* (Three Counties Press, 2006).

The Artist

Leila Canney was born in Galway City but has lived in Athlone since 1972. Though self-taught as an artist she has attended regular workshops in the Burren and elsewhere.

Leila specialises in watercolour painting and concentrates on landscapes with an emphasis on scenes from the bog-lands and waterways of her adopted Midlands. She is a founder member of both Athlone Arts Group and the Midland Watercolour Society. Leila has exhibited widely, has had work accepted for the Oireachtais Exhibition and has held solo shows in Galway, Sligo, Mayo and Athlone.

Westmeath County Council commissioned her to paint six scenes for their calendar in 1994 and these are on permanent exhibition in the County Buildings in Mullingar. Leila is married to Billy Comber a native of Athlone. They have three adult children, sons John and Philip and daughter Jennifer and two grandchildren, Sean and Maureen. Leila works from her home in Coosan, Athlone.

Contents

Welcome to Athlone   7

Paintings and Stories from Athlone

Moored on the Shannon	14
Custume Place	16
Civic Offices and Athlone Town Centre	18
The Eel Nets	20
The Weir from Burgess Park	22
Athlone Castle	24
Main Street and Sean's Bar	26
The Lock Gates	28
Fry Place	30
Bastion Street	32
Connaught Street	34
The Railway Bridge and Barges	36
Athlone Canal and Talbot Avenue	38
Gorry Bog	40
Clonown	42
Drum Farmyard	44
The Hill of Berries	46
Athlone Golf Club, Hodson Bay	48
Temple Island	50
Lough Ree Yacht Club	52
The Pigeon House, Waterston	54
Glasson Village	56
Glasson Golf and Country Club	58
Portlick Walk	60
Mill on the Inny	62
Moydrum Bog	64
Farmhouse at Ballinahowen	66
Temple Finghin and Round Tower, Clonmacnoise	68
The Nuns' Church, Clonmacnoise	70
Athlone Skyline from Clonown	72

Athlone through the Ages   75

A Few Famous Athlonians   87

Welcome to Athlone

At school we were told that Athlone was at the centre of the 'saucer' of Ireland and that, I have often thought, was not a bad description at all. Obviously if rain falls on a saucer it will run down the sloped sides and gather in the centre. But the 'saucer' that we are living on is an organic saucer with its own complex system of drainage and percolation.

Athlone town lies in the very centre of Ireland, having grown up at a crossing point (or ford) on the River Shannon. The great Irish naturalist Robert Lloyd Praeger described it well when he wrote '*Ancient crumplings of the Earth's crust have resulted in the formation of mountain ranges in the coastal regions, leaving a broad low plain in the centre*'. Apart from the Shannon and its tributaries we have more than our fair share of wet bogs lying to the east and west of Athlone. The Midlands, it must be said, are famous (or infamous) for their vast expanses of peat-bogs.

The hinterland of Athlone is not prime farming land. However, Athlone was once the centre of a thriving seed potato trade and farmers have found that the peaty soil is also an ideal medium for growing carrots and other root crops. The Shannon callows, which form a unique habitat for wintering wild-fowl and wading birds and for the now rare summer visitor the corncrake, also provide a rich agricultural asset to the farmers of the area. I suppose to call it a 'rich agricultural asset' might be something of an exaggeration because the land is liable to flooding (and not only in the winter) and thus farming on the callows can be a precarious proposition. However in a good summer the hay yield from these fields, which have been fertilised by the winter floods, can be impressive. The fields also provide excellent summer grazing for cattle.

The underlying rock around Athlone is a carboniferous limestone and on top of this is a further limestone glacial drift and esker ridges of sandy moraine material – much of it

Welcome to Athlone

calcareous. If you would like to learn more about the geology of our Midland landscape read Frank Mitchell and Michael Ryan's book *Reading the Irish Landscape*.

Athlone (ÁthLuain): the Ford of Luan

The earliest name for the settlement, which we now know as Athlone, at a safe fording-point on the middle Shannon is *An Sean Áth Mor* (or The Great Ford of Antiquity). By the tenth century the ford was known as ÁthLuain with the anglicised form Athlone first recorded in a document of 1214.

An obvious question is who or what was 'Luan'. Unfortunately there is no easy answer to this question. Several versions of the derivation of the name have been recorded from early Irish literature. Among the more popular ones are the following:

The first is to be found in the Dindshenchus of *Snám Da En* (Swim two birds) a stretch of the Shannon near Clonmacnois:

'Estiu, wife of Nár, had a lover Buide, son of Derg, who used to come with his foster-brother Luan in the form of a bird to visit Estiu. The magic of their song lulled all around to sleep so that Buide could enjoy the company of Estiu undisturbed. The jealous husband, Nár, asked a druid about what was happening and the druid revealed the secret to him. Nár set out for the Shannon and shot the two birds (Buide and Luan) with one cast.

Estiu who witnessed this act died of grief at Mág Esten (the modern Moystown) near Shannon Harbour. Luan, though injured, managed to fly north to the ford where he died. The ford is named after him: ÁthLuain.'

A second version concerns an event in a great battle fought between the men of Connacht and the men of Ulster before the destruction of Dá Chogás Hostel, Luan son of Suanach was slain and from him ÁthLuain was named.

A third version comes from the great epic tale The Cattle Raid of Cooley *(Táin Bo Cualigne)*. Here we learn that the brown bull of Cooley killed the white-horned bull of Mág Ai and tossed his carcass into the lake near Rathcroghan but carried his loin (or haunch) and his liver away on his horns. Returning to the north he stooped to take a drink from the Shannon and dropped the loin of the white-horned bull. The place where it was dropped was named after the 'lon' or haunch: hence ÁthLuain.

A popular version of the naming of Athlone concerns *Luan Mac Luighdeach* (or Luan the son of Lewy) our first entrepreneur who, according to tradition, lived at the close of the first century. It has been suggested that he kept his hostelry on the bank of the river and was frequently called upon to guide travellers across the rapids. In time the crossing point became known as ÁthLuain – or the ford of Luan.

There are other versions which suggest that the 'Luan' element is derived from *luna,* the Latin word for the moon, and that ÁthLuain may mean the ford of the moon or perhaps the ford of the moon-worshippers. So you might well ask was Luan the enchanted foster-brother of Buide; a slain warrior; a loin of the white-horned bull of Mág Ai or Athlone's first recorded publican and entrepreneur – well, as the saying goes "you pays your money and you takes your chance".

ATHLONE: THE HEART OF IRELAND

In modern times Athlone has been described in several different ways. To some it is 'The Gateway to the West', to others 'The Capital of the Midlands', and it certainly lives up to both of these titles. However, my favourite name is 'Athlone: the heart of Ireland', a name which was first used in tourist brochures over eighty years ago.

Athlone enjoys a pivotal location in terms of the road and rail network of Ireland. While the town grew up on an ancient crossing point and enjoyed a strategic importance unparalleled in the Midlands today three major bridges cross the Shannon providing linkages for road and rail traffic from east to west. The Shannon-Erne waterway provides a further artery of communication linking Limerick and the Midlands, with the North of Ireland. Because of its central location Athlone has experienced great growth and has become a major base for national conferences and meetings.

A TOWN DIVIDED

The river Shannon divides the town of Athlone into two parishes, two dioceses, two counties and two provinces. The two Catholic parishes in Athlone are St Mary's, to the east which is in the dioceses of Ardagh and Clonmacnoise and St Peter's, to the west which is in Elphin. The suburban area west of Athlone belongs in County Roscommon and the province of Connaught while Athlone town belongs in County Westmeath and the province of Leinster. Until the Local Government Act of 1899 all of Athlone west of the Shannon was considered to be in County Roscommon but for administrative purposes the urban area west of Athlone has since been considered as belonging to County Westmeath.

No matter which side of Athlone you grew up in you will surely have heard people described as being from 'the far side'. For those living on the Leinster side those in Connaught were living 'on the far side' and for those living on the Connaught side those living in Leinster were from 'the far side'.

Welcome to Athlone

The gentle rivalry between the two sides of Athlone has given rise to many talks and debates over the years. Several years ago a researcher from RTE arranged to meet me to talk about my contribution to a magazine-type programme which they were then planning. She explained that it would be a light-hearted look at the town and its history.

"What type of topics would you hope to cover?" I asked. "Oh, perhaps about the differences between the two sides of town – which side is the poor relation and that sort of thing." I was a bit taken aback and obviously reluctant because at that time I was newly married, and though reared on the Leinster side, and schooled on both sides, I had married a girl from the 'far side' and was living in Connaught. The researcher considered I would be ideally placed to talk on the subject but I certainly didn't want to alienate anyone, not least my new in-laws, with anything I might have to say. I told the researcher that I thought that this topic was old hat and that perhaps it was time to take a more historical look at the town. I had recently got a copy of a 1784 map of Athlone and produced it to try to convince her. The researcher asked me to talk her through it, which I gladly did.

"This is the Leinster side I said – here is the town wall, the site of the two gate-houses, an old monastery outside the town walls, the parish church, and the main street. And this is the old town bridge – the bridge that saw service during the sieges of 1690 and 1691 and even if Athlone was divided by the Shannon it was united by this bridge. Beyond it is the Connaught side – starting with the castle and a series of streets radiating out from it. Here is the army barracks occupying the same site as it does today…"

"Sorry" the researcher interjected – "where is the town wall on the Connaught side?"

"They didn't really have a wall on the far side," I said, "they just had some sort of defensive ditch".

"Oh," she said. "Do you think the rivalry between the two sides of the town goes back to the time of the building of the town wall?" I felt almost ready to admit defeat.

So when did this rivalry start? Who knows? I do know that the great Elizabethan bridge of 1567 had a monument built into it with several stone tablets displayed on it. Some of these stones are lying in the vaults of the National Museum. There was also a stone tablet, known as the 'mearing stone' which was in the centre of the bridge but is now to be found in St Mary's Church of Ireland. This marked the old boundary between the counties of Westmeath and Roscommon and there is even a story told that there was also another stone tablet which read

'Here civilisation ends and barbarism begins'. Fortunately we do not know for sure whether it was the civilisation or the barbarism which was to be found on the Leinster side of the bridge. It is, as they say, all a matter of perspective.

ATHLONE: A GARRISON TOWN

Athlone has been seen as having strategic importance since the twelfth century at least. It became established as a garrison town in the late seventeenth century in the aftermath of the famous Siege of Athlone. From about 1697 a military barracks existed in Athlone on the site still occupied by Custume Barracks today.

Over the centuries countless regiments of the British Army have served here – the Royal Artillery, The Gordon Highlanders, The Royal Irish Fusiliers, The Royal Scots, The Buffs and The Connaught Rangers to name but a few. To date nobody has attempted to undertake an indepth sociological study on the effects of the military presence in Athlone and its benefits to local society. Certainly the garrison introduced several sporting and cultural events to Athlone. Members of the garrison were to the fore in sailing, rugby, soccer and golf. In terms of music and entertainment the presence of military bands over a period of several hundred years has obviously helped to shape the musical life of Athlone. The same is true for theatricals as the earliest recorded performances were associated with garrison theatre.

A proud moment in the history of Athlone took place in February 1922 when the Union Jack which had flown over Athlone castle for many years was replaced by a tricolour. Men, women and children lined the streets to watch the withdrawal of the British troops from Victoria Barracks and the introduction of the fledgling National Army of the Free State under the command of Col Tony Lawlor to the barracks which was then re-named Custume Barracks.

A TOWN OF SPIRES

The first time visitor to Athlone is often struck by the number of churches and spires to be seen. Part of the reason for this is, of course, that Athlone has two parishes and each parish has its own church or churches. Another legacy of the garrison to Athlone is that it gave us a healthy spread of religious beliefs with several churches flourishing here in the 19th Century.

In terms of Catholic churches we have St Anthony's Friary which was opened in 1931 but the Franciscans have had a continuous presence in Athlone since about 1240. On the Leinster side we also have St Mary's Church, architect John Bourke, built in 1862 and the beautiful modern the church of Our Lady Queen of Peace in Coosan designed by local architect Noel F. Heavey. In St Peter's parish we have the magnificent church of SS Peter & Paul, architect Ralph Byrne, which overlooks the bridge and the Shannon. There are two other parish

Welcome to Athlone

churches in Clonown (built 1965, Noel F. Heavey architect) and Drum where the church was built in the 1870s and modernised in 1964. The Society of Pius X has its Catholic church in Ganly Lane in a former Church of Ireland building and regular Tridentine mass services are held here.

St Mary's Church of Ireland, built in 1827, enjoys a town centre location and is one of the most interesting buildings in Athlone. The Church of Ireland originally had churches on both sides of the town but these were amalgamated and St Peter's Church of Ireland closed in the 1940s. There is a Methodist church on Northgate Street which was built to the design of A.J. Jones in 1862 and a modern Baptist chapel on Battery Road. In the past we also had an active Presbyterian community with their own church on the docks which was built in 1860 and served for more than a hundred years.

ATHLONE TODAY

Athlone today reflects a thousand years of growth. The Castle still stands guarding the crossing point of the Shannon, however today it is a tourist attraction rather than a military fortress. The Shannon has three bridges spanning it at Athlone – the town bridge which was completed in 1844, the railway bridge which was completed in 1851 and 'Shannon Way', the new bridge which was opened in 1991 as part of the Athlone Relief Road project.

The transport infrastructure is excellent. We have a choice of commercial bus services to Galway, Dublin and direct to Dublin airport as well as a wide choice of bus destinations around Ireland. The rail network has direct services to Dublin, Galway and Westport. The improvement in the road network has resulted in faster journey times between Athlone and Dublin, and today many workers and some students commute between Dublin and Athlone on a daily basis.

The twentieth century witnessed a great rise in educational opportunities. Athlone was quick to adopt the Technical Education Act of 1899 and a Technical School was established in Garden Vale in 1902. The Marist Brothers and La Sainte Union sisters continued to look after the educational needs of the children of Athlone offering both primary and secondary education. In St Peter's parish girls were educated up to and including secondary level in St Peter's convent school which, like Our Lady's Bower, offered both day-school and boarding option. In the 1960s St Aloysius College a diocesan school of the Elphin diocese was founded by Fr John Feeney. Later the secondary school from St. Peter's transferred to St Joseph's College, Summerhill.

In the 1970s Athlone got its first third level educational establishment in the form of Athlone Regional Technical College. Now over thirty years later, as Athlone Institute of Technology, it is a major third level college serving the Midlands and offering a wide range of courses at certificate, diploma and degree level. The College has Schools of Business, Humanities, Science and Engineering and attracts a wide range of students from at home and abroad.

The housing stock in Athlone has increased exponentially in recent years. Housing estates which were once considered to be on the outskirts have now been absorbed into the town and there is great choice in terms of available housing and apartment units.

Employment prospects are good with a wide range of industries, a large military barracks, government offices including the examination branch of the Department of Education, and a great deal of commercial activity and retail outlets. The hospitality sector is also a great source of local employment.

The cultural life of Athlone is catered for in many ways. The town has no fewer than three theatres the largest of which, The Dean Crowe Theatre, was refurbished and extended in recent years. The theatre is the venue for the All Ireland Drama Festival. Athlone also has an annual Literary Festival. Live music is catered for in The Dean Crowe Theatre and in several of the hotels. Athlone has had a public library for over fifty years and it has a number of bookshops.

When it comes to sport Athlone is well endowed with clubs and venues. The three catalysts to the growth of sport have been the development of a major Sports Centre by Athlone Town Council, and the contribution of both Athlone IT and Custume Barracks to sport over the years. The Regional Sports Centre at Ballymahon Road offers swimming pool, gym and all weather pitches. Nearby is the new soccer stadium for Athlone Town FC; the GAA has their own grounds and clubhouse as does the Buccaneers Rugby club. Golf is still alive and well with courses at Hodson Bay, Glasson and Mount Temple. Boxing which was once very big in Athlone is making a come-back and predictions are that athletics will grow with the development of a track at Athlone I.T.

In recent years Athlone has taken on a very cosmopolitan air with the arrival of new residents from Europe, Africa and elsewhere. The largest group of non Irish nationals is the Polish community. No longer is Athlone the typical suburban small town depicted by local author John Broderick in his novels where everyone knew everyone else. Athlone has come a long way from the small town mentality which prevailed here fifty years ago. Today Athlone displays an outward sign of confidence and in all but name it has become a city. There have been local initiatives to have Athlone declared a city – but life in Athlone has many of the benefits but few of the disadvantages of city life, and the future looks bright for Athlone.

Quite simply the River Shannon and its natural fording point is the raison d'etre of Athlone. Across the world one of the most common reasons for the growth of a town has traditionally been the ease of access to fresh water.

The Shannon is the largest river in these islands meandering for over two hundred miles in length from its source in County Leitrim to Limerick and outwards to its broad estuary which lies between counties Clare and Kerry. There are those who claim that the Shannon is a ridiculously large river for such a small island but we can't do much about that. It is so large that it almost cuts the island of Ireland in two and it forms the boundary between the ancient provinces of Leinster and Connaught. Long before the arrival of the Normans those who wished to cross the country from east to west had to find a way across the Shannon which, prior to the Shannon Navigation works, was a much wider and more untamed waterway.

The crossing point at AthLuain was ideally placed as the ancient highway, An Sli Mor, was carried on an esker ridge which created the ford as it crossed the Shannon. For a thousand years at least, Athlone has enjoyed a symbiotic relationship with the Shannon. It was the Shannon which endowed Athlone with its strategic significance and which enabled generations of Athlonians to bring goods in and out of Athlone by barge. From the earliest times the Shannon has been a source of food and water. It is said that in the nineteenth century salmon was so common at Athlone that many deeds of apprenticeship carried the phrase regarding food that the apprentice was not to be served salmon more than twice or three times in a week.

The Shannon provided the water for industry in the nineteenth century, a highway of communication for transport and pleasure (including the great Shannon steamers of the Victorian era) and today it continues to provide endless opportunities for recreation including fishing, swimming, sailing and cruising – without the Shannon there would be no Athlone.

Moored on the Shannon

The Provincial Bank opened its doors as the first commercial bank in Athlone in 1827. It was then located on the corner of Northgate Street opposite the old Tholsel or Market House. By coincidence part of the original site is now occupied by a branch of National Irish Bank. The Provincial Bank attracted many local investors and had two local directors. In 1839 during the night of the Big Wind the Provincial Bank lost *'an immensity of slates'*.

The only banknote ever issued from Athlone was a Provincial Bank of Ireland £1 note which was issued in 1839. It promised to pay the bearer *'on demand one pound British at Athlone'*. These notes carried the head of Queen Victoria and were authenticated by being individually signed, numbered and dated by the local bank manager. The notes were printed in Britain by an American printer, Jacob Perkins, the man who printed the first adhesive postage stamps in 1840.

The new town bridge was completed in 1844. Unlike the earlier bridge which crossed the river south of Athlone Castle the new bridge took a route which cut through the small market area in front of the Tholsel. It ran north of the castle thus putting the Provincial Bank on the great new highway to the West. In the 1850s Athlone witnessed a new era of growth. Encouraged by the development of the Athlone Woollen Mills and a wave of building activity including a second railway station and a new parish church for St. Mary's parish the Provincial Bank decided to place an even greater confidence in its Athlone operation by building a new purpose built bank in Custume Place. The architect appointed was William G. Murray of Dublin and the new bank, which was completed by 1860, ranks as one of the most impressive Victorian buildings in Athlone.

The laneway, which runs beneath the footbridge to the river, and indeed the laneway which once connected that laneway with Malthouse Lane, were once called Hatter's Lane. The name relates to the ancient craft of felt-hat making which was carried on here in the eighteenth and early nineteenth centuries.

Athlone Workhouse

Custume Place

Many people look on 1991 as a pivotal year in the modern history of Athlone. That year, Athlone Urban District Council spearheaded the efforts to mark the Tercentenary of the Siege of Athlone. Two major infrastructural changes came to fruition: Athlone Castle re-opened with a state-of-the-art Visitor Centre and the Athlone Relief Road was opened. The Tercentenary celebrations helped to create a renewed sense of civic pride in Athlone.

As Athlone prepared to enter the new millennium great things were promised for the town. The local authorities, Westmeath County Council and Athlone Town Council revealed plans to build a new Civic Centre and Library for Athlone. As a result of open competition the task of designing this landmark building was awarded to a London based firm Keith Williams Architects. The result was an amazing modern building, built by John Sisk & Son, which speaks of the great confidence in the future of Athlone. The Civic Centre opened in September 2004 and included offices for Athlone Town Council and Westmeath County Council, an impressive Council Chamber and The Aidan Heavey Public Library.

The Office Centre, Mardyke Street

The Aidan Heavey Library also houses the prestigious Aidan Heavey Collection, a superb private library donated to his home town by Athlone born philanthropist, Aidan Heavey and his Cork born wife Maureen (nee O'Sullivan). This library of almost 20,000 items of Irish interest attracts serious scholars to Athlone because of the extraordinary range of unique and rare items which it contains.

The adjacent Town Centre development, completed in 2007-08 was developed by Gallico Developers and is a further indication of confidence in the future of Athlone. This most attractive complex of buildings, to the design of Murray O'Laoire Architects, of Dublin wraps around the Civic Centre and utilises the former Royal Hoey Hotel site, together with the old ESB site to provide a two-storey shopping mall, a new town-centre hotel The Athlone Sheraton Hotel (our first high rise building) and residential units which will help to inject life into the heart of Athlone. This is the new Athlone!

Civic Offices and Athlone Town Centre

It must surely have been the fact that Paul Henry's grandparents lived in Athlone that prompted him to paint a local scene. He painted a view of the eel nets at Athlone which now hangs in Athlone Library. It was donated to the library service by the novelist John Broderick.

Historians are in agreement that eel fishing is our oldest commercial activity. According to Archdall, writing in 1786, Edward I granted the *'weirs and fisheries'* of Athlone to the monks of St. Peter's Abbey. In 1290 Prior Gilbert received *forty shillings in silver'* as compensation for the losses they had sustained in their fish pool because of the polluting effect of the royal mill. Another citizen Thomas de Pykering had weirs at Athlone and in accounts for 30th July 1293 he accounted for the sum of £4.16s.0d. *'out of 3,600 eels sold at Athlone'* representing a selling price of about three-pence per eel.

In a classic nineteenth century book on fishing the authors writes of his experiences in Athlone:

> 'There were, indeed, eels – and in such abundance, exposed at every shop, whiskey-hovel, or lodging window – eels of three, four or five pounds, which would seem to imply that they constituted the chief food of the people. This turned out to be the fact. These animals descend the Shannon in such multitudes, that, in the autumn, after the flood, the rapids and falls in the narrow part of the river need only be crossed by a purse net, and tons worth of eels are taken in one night.'

The eel weirs consist of a series of posts and nets stretching across the river from the docks towards the Strand, with a pass on the Leinster side, traditionally called 'The Queen's Pass'. This allows some eels to negotiate the river unhindered. The eel weirs add greatly to the atmospheric look of the river in winter. The eel fisheries are controlled by the E.S.B. and many of the eels caught in Athlone are destined for the continental market.

The Eel Nets

The sound of the weir is perhaps the most quintessential sound of the Shannon at Athlone. On quiet nights it can be heard from the streets of the town giving its watery benediction to one and all. Like all water features the weir changes according to the season. At the height of winter, when the Shannon is in flood, the weir virtually disappears under water becoming little more than a ridge running from Burgess Park to the sluice gates at the docks. In spring and autumn the weir is at its most glorious with the water cascading noisily over it. And in the summer, especially during periods of drought, the weir becomes dry and is a favourite roosting place for a variety of water-birds including black-headed gulls and the grey-heron.

This beautiful 'u' shaped weir-wall was built as part of the Shannon Navigation works of the 1840s. It lends a great sense of grace to views of Athlone from the south but spare a thought for the men who worked on this and other aspects of this great project. There was little joy for those who laboured at deepening the river bed and building features such as the weir. A contemporary account is worth quoting:

> *'The long promised works on the Shannon improvements at Athlone commenced on Monday when 700 men were employed. The works consist of deepening the bed of the river and clearing away the remains of the ancient bridge. A good deal of disappointment was expressed by the large numbers who were rejected, many of the starving creatures having travelled long distances in the hope of being employed. On Friday the number of hands was increased to 1,000. According to a correspondent the whips of the overseers and gangers were in constant requisition and the view from the bridge would remind you of the manner in which the Negroes of America are kept at work.'*

As a child growing up in the 1960s I saw several salmon climbing, or attempting to climb, the weir and wondered why they never seem to find the salmon pass almost mid-way along its length. Today salmon are a rare sight on the Shannon at Athlone.

The Weir from Burgess Park

The Anglo-Norman town grew up around the castle which was built at the behest of King John of England. Though not the first castle to be built at Athlone this castle has endured like no other. Looking at it today it incorporates elements of the castle of 1210 together with various additions and alterations which were made in response to the changing nature of warfare. It has many of the characteristics of a Napoleonic fortification as it was at this time that it was last remodelled. That is until recent times when its function changed from warfare to tourism.

Over the centuries it was the nucleus of the Anglo-Norman settlement, a stronghold of the rival local families the Dillons and the O'Kelly's, the seat of the Court of Claims, the residence of the President of Connaught and the Jacobite stronghold during the sieges of Athlone before becoming an integral part of the military barrack complex. It was to remain part of the garrison for almost three hundred years.

In 1967 the Old Athlone Society established a museum in the castle with an excellent range of exhibits relating to Athlone and its environs and also to folk-life in the district. Two years later when the military left the castle it was handed over to the Office of Public Works and the central keep became a National Monument.

In 1991 to mark the Tercentenary of the Siege of Athlone the castle became the foremost visitor attraction in Athlone. Athlone Town Council (then Athlone UDC) made a major investment in the castle creating a multi-faceted Visitor Centre. Here together with the museum were audio-visual presentations on the castle, the Siege of Athlone, John McCormack, the military history of Athlone and the River Shannon. A new reception area was built linking two of the old buildings. Bord Failte also invested in the refurbishment of an old building to create a modern Tourist Office for Athlone.

Now as the castle approaches its 800th anniversary in 2010 there are plans afoot to upgrade the facilities once again and bring to bring the standards of interpretation and display in line with the visitor expectations of the twenty-first century.

Athlone Castle

The name Main Street is found in many towns and is frequently the butt of jokes. Someone asks, "Is this Main Street?" only to get the reply, "Well, have you ever seen meaner?" In Athlone the visitor is often confused by the name Main Street because today this seems like a quite back-water. Today Main Street is part of the 'Left Bank' area of Athlone associated with restaurants, pubs, craft shops and a leisurely pace of life but this was not always the case.

Before the Shannon Navigation works of the 1840s and the building of a new bridge across the Shannon, all road traffic coming through Athlone from east to west came through Church Street, down Bridge Street across the old bridge and straight into Main Street then going through High Street, Bastion Street, O'Connell Street and Connaught Street before crossing the Batteries to join up with the road to Galway.

Sean's Bar has a most attractive shop-front with its four Ionic columns; these are not original, having once adorned Gill's in O'Connell Street, Dublin. The pub has a long and distinguished history – it has been suggested that it may have stood here during the siege of 1691. Certainly in the eighteenth century the predecessor of Sean's Bar, the Sign of the Three Blackamoor Heads was one of the best known inns of Athlone. In 1738, Mark Begg, the proprietor of the inn, started the first stage coach service from Athlone to Dublin.

Restoration of the neighbouring premises some years ago revealed an old gateway which gave access to the yard for the stabling of horses. Sean's Bar as it stands is a building of three storeys but the third storey is obviously a later addition. Renovation work which was carried out in 1970 revealed a mud and wattle wall creating a division between rooms on the first floor. A section of this wickerwork partition has been preserved and can be seen on the premises. Sean's Bar has been included in countless guide books and travelogues because of its old world charm and legendary hospitality.

Main Street and Sean's Bar

The area around the docks in Athlone is a tranquil place beloved of fishermen and sightseers alike. Many a pike-fisherman has landed a more than decent pike by casting a line into the frothy waters below the sluices and many a trout fisherman has landed a good brown-trout from the placid waters above the sluices. Generations of school-boys, myself included in my day, have tantalised themselves and the perch by dangling hooked-worms from the lock-gates or from the dock walls.

Commenced in 1845 but not completed for more than three years the building of the lock was one of the more difficult aspects of the Shannon navigation works of the 1840s. If Harry Rice is correct in saying that labourers received *'sixpence a day for a six day week'* then it can hardly be surprising that a workers strike occurred which slowed down the progress of the scheme.

In the 1840s those designing the lock could never imagine a time when the bulk of goods arriving in Athlone were not going to arrive by barge. The capacity of the lock was dictated to by the size and quantity of barges which weekly plied the Shannon. Then years later the railway came to town and the wide capacious lock seemed something of an extravagance.

In the nineteenth century the area around the docks was a hive of industrial activity with a distillery, a furniture factory and a busy saw-mill providing great employment prospects for the men of Athlone. Today the docks has become almost entirely residential with many homes and apartments enjoying unrivalled views of the Shannon.

When I was a child I loved to watch Mr Hewitt the lock-keeper and his co-worker, Sean Fitzpatrick, manually opening and closing the lock-gates. Today the locks are opened and closed at the flick of a switch but even so they are still no less fascinating to watch.

The Lock Gates

Fry Place is a fine Regency terrace which takes its name from a family named Fry who settled here in 1744. They continued to be identified with life in the town until the 1830s. Fry Place was built in 1806 on the site of the 'Mansion House' an old building which was probably semi-fortified. The numbering system on this terrace reads from right to left. The first occupant of No 1 was a Thomas Fallon. It was later a hardware shop until 1922 when the Irish National Foresters moved here from King Street. They restored the magnificent facade in the 1980s before quietly closing the premises which were taken over by Michael Cuddy, accountant on the upper floors and Pavarotti's Restaurant on the ground floor.

No 2 was occupied by John Walker a merchant until 1824. It was later the premises of John Doyle grocer. Messrs Yates occupied it from 1862 and in 1924 it became Elliot's. The Elliots ran a popular business here for almost fifty years. It later became the Angler's Rest lounge bar and then 'Yates'. It has been vacant for some time.

No 3 was always a residential premises. In 1816 it was the home of John O'Beirne a well known local distiller. By 1886 it was the residence of Dr. Charles Joseph McCormack, a local doctor, and in more recent times it was the residence of the Mulligan family before being amalgamated with No 4 to accommodate the Left Bank Restaurant.

No 4 was originally a residence for a senior officer of the Board of Ordnance. It later became a grocery shop and bar. In January 1896 Mr O'Ferrall acquired the premises and opened for business as publican and auctioneer. In 1954 Joseph McFarland took over but later transferred their business to Garden Vale. Following major renovations the award winning Left Bank Bistro moved from Bastion Street to the ground floor of 3 and 4 Fry Place bringing a very welcome injection of life to these pivotal buildings.

Fry Place

A deed of 1756 refers to this short street as 'Royal Bastion' but during the first Ordnance Survey and for the purposes of Griffith's Valuations it was considered as part of Wentworth Street (the modern O'Connell Street). This is one of the few street-names on the Connaught side of Athlone which recalls the town fortifications. Obviously there was once a bastion at this point on the defensive ditch which protected the western boundary of the town.

It was not until a revision of the Ordnance Survey in 1874 that Bastion Street got the recognition it deserved. One of the great characters of Bastion Street was Michael Kilkelly, the son of a local shopkeeper James Kilkelly. He was born during Famine times and lived here until his death in 1940, at age of ninety-three. He became involved in the family business at a very early age due to the early death of his father.

Michael Kilkelly did more than anyone else of his generation to promote and foster a love of music in Athlone. He was choir-master of the old St Peter's Church (the present Dean Crowe Theatre) and was involved in brass-bands, quartets and other musical activities in the town. He was a boyhood friend of T. P. O'Connor's, as both had attended Summerhill College in Athlone, before it moved to Sligo. However he is perhaps best remembered for his early encouragement of John McCormack, a fellow Athlonian with whom a lifelong friendship endured.

Apart from his great love of music Michael Kilkelly was also passionate about politics. A staunch supporter of both Parnell and the Land League movement he was a local organiser for both movements in Athlone. He even spoke from the same platform as Parnell himself. He served on the old Town Commissioners and later the Urban Council and through a series of articles penned for *The Westmeath Independent* in the 1930s he left us a legacy of wonderfully evocative social commentaries which put flesh on the otherwise dry bones of local history. Today his great granddaughter runs the Bastion Gallery, while her brothers run Garbz, a fashion shop next-door.

Bastion Street

Athlone grew up around the Castle and the crossing point of the river. Gradually the town expanded eastwards but by medieval times there was also a thriving market-town west of the Shannon. The medieval fortifications encompassed a tight nucleus on the Connaught side from the river through Bastion Street and Queen Street, through the land on which the Barracks now stands and back to the river at the present Promenade. Beyond this all else was country with green fields and perhaps a scattering of cabins where Connaught Street is now.

So what is so special about Connaught Street? Unlike Church Street where the merchant classes set up shop, Connaught Street was very much an Irish street closely linked to successful farming families of south Roscommon. Many of those who formerly brought their produce to market in Athlone eventually set up in business in this street.

The earliest recorded mention of the name 'Connaught Street' is on a deed of 1715 and by the time the Ranelagh Estate map of 1784 was drawn the street was well established. It probably developed in tandem with the eighteenth century coach road. Once the coach service extended to the west this area was opened up and developed. Inns sprung up; stalls and shops moved out from the crowded area around the Castle and private residences were built. The last stage-coach, a Bianconi stage, ran in 1850 and by then Connaught Street had become an important street in its own right. Before the creation of the Accommodation Road in the 1850s road traffic to the West travelled via Connaught Street, across the Batteries and joined the Galway Road at Halls Bridge.

In the nineteenth century and for much of the twentieth century Connaught Street was one of the great shopping streets in Athlone. It has recently experienced great regeneration and is regaining its status in terms of both residential and commercial development. The redbrick premises which houses 'A Slice of Life' was once Broderick's Bakery. Connaught Street features heavily in the Athlone novels of John Broderick (1924-1989), a member of the Broderick family of Connaught Street.

Connaught Street

The coming of the railway to Athlone was one of the most significant developments of the nineteenth century. Today we take so much for granted but in terms of civil engineering projects the laying of the railway line from Dublin to Galway was an incredible achievement by any standards. The first railway line to arrive in Athlone was an extension of the Midland Great Western Railway from Mullingar – sadly in recent years this line has been closed.

As the railway approached Athlone the railway company had to tackle the obstacle of crossing the Shannon. The work of designing a railway bridge fell to Mr G. W. Hemans a famous railway engineer and the son of an equally famous mother, Mrs Felicia Dorothea Hemans. It was Mrs Hemans, a noted Victorian poet, who penned the immortal lines:

> 'The boy stood on the burning deck
> Whence all but he had fled'

George W. Hemans designed this majestic bridge on the bowstring and lattice principle. The contract for the ironwork was given to Fox Henderson and Company and it was built under the supervision of the great railway contractor William Dargan. The bridge is supported on twelve cylindrical pillars and is 560 feet in length. It consists of two spans of 175 feet and two of 40 feet each. Up to the mid 1930s the opening central span, which operated on a swivel basis, was opened twice a year to accommodate yachts with high superstructures which were participating in the regatta on Lough Ree.

Today there are a number of barges moored near the bridge – these are the homes of Shannon-lovers who chose to live on the river. It was the coming of the railway which first threatened the business of the barges. These were used to transport goods to and from Athlone by river and canal. However the barge traffic survived for another century in competition with the railway. Among the commodities traditionally transported by barge were the barrels of porter from the Guinness Brewery. These were delivered to the Guinness Store which once stood just below the town bridge on the west bank of the river.

The Railway Bridge and Barges

Athlone Canal and Talbot Avenue

Athlone Canal which is approximately a mile in length was the original Athlone 'by-pass'. Because of the glacial deposit in the bed of the Shannon at Athlone the river was never navigable through Athlone. When some of our earliest tourists, the Vikings, arrived, they had to put their long-boats on their shoulders to convey them across country dropping them north or south of the town. Carrying a boat or dug-out canoe is not exactly a favourite holiday pastime so in order to keep the tourists, and indeed the natives, happy, a solution had to be found to the navigation problem. By the eighteenth century serious thoughts were given to the prospect of making the Shannon navigable through Athlone.

In January 1757 the people of Athlone were informed that land was being acquired for cutting a canal. In July that year Thomas Omer, a Dutch engineer arrived in Athlone to inspect the proposed route. He approved and very soon the live register was seasonally adjusted with 325 men gaining employment cutting the canal and building the road which we now know as The Magazine Road.

Originally there were two locks – one a full lock near the present Mick McQuaid's Bridge and the other a guard lock near the footbridge leading to the Batteries. The canal was designed for cots and barges propelled by sail. The benefit to the town was the ease of bringing commercial cargoes into Athlone by water.

Below the town a private harbour, St Peter's Port, was developed. The canal enjoyed a very chequered career. By 1801 the lock was missing and the banks were in disrepair. Within a decade £50,000 was spent on improving the canal to allow it to accommodate large barges.

The Shannon Navigation works of the 1840s negated the need for this canal. It soon became a quiet backwater and the lock was used to power a mill. At first this was a corn mill and later a Woollen Mill owned by Heatons. In 1982 an abandonment order was signed releasing the Commissioners of Public Work from their duty to maintain the middle section of the canal between the Galway Road and Mick McQuaid's bridge and much of this section has been piped and filled in.

The kiss of the sun for pardon
The song of the birds for mirth
One is nearer God's heart in a garden
Than anywhere else on earth

The poet who penned these immortal lines was Dorothy Frances Gurney. Apart from the fact that she was born in 1858 and died in 1932 I know nothing of her life. I assume that apart from being a poet she was also a keen gardener. But she was obviously not Irish because if she were both Irish and a poet she would have realised that God's garden is not the formal garden of the herbaceous borders and neat bean rows. To me God's garden is a place of infinite colour and sound and texture and serenity. God's garden is not our garden. God's garden does not need garden gnomes or conservatories or patios or gazeboes. God's garden is constantly evolving and manages with or without the intervention of man.

It is up to each of us to find God's garden for ourselves. It is the place in which we always feel welcome. It is the place to which we can come bringing the burdens of life with us knowing that we will leave with a lighter heart. It is the place where we can choose to be alone with our thoughts or to share this beauty with a friend or friends. For me God's garden is the bog. Not just any bog …though any bog would do.

Bog Cotton

I have my own stretch of bog in Clonown. I don't own it but I have made it my own. Sometimes a lazy tractor will purr across the landscape to draw home the turf, sometimes the rivulets which drain the upper layer of bog will gurgle melodiously as if playing out a symphony and sometimes the only sound will be the sound of silence; a sound one strains to hear only to realise that it is in fact the sound of the absence of sound. Around Athlone we have no shortage of bogs – you don't have to be a poet or artist to appreciate them!

Gorry Bog

Clonown is an ancient village in the barony of Athlone, Co. Roscommon. It does not now have a shop, pub or post-office but it does have a thriving close-knit community, a national school which is second to none and new houses which are springing up with great rapidity. When the old church, built c 1825, was being converted into a Community Centre c 1970 a fragment of an early Christian grave slab (possibly of eighth century date) and of the Clonmacnoise type, was discovered in a wall behind the altar. It was a gentle reminder that Christianity had come to Clonown before ever St Ciaran founded his beautiful monastery of Clonmacnoise in 545 AD.

Adjacent to the Community Centre is the site of the ancient monastery of Clonown where, according to tradition, seven bishops reigned. One of these was St Eamhain, a sixth century cleric who died in 535 AD. According to the ancient annals Clonown (or its monastery) was plundered by the O'Briens in 1089 and it seems to fade out of history soon after that. In fields around the old church traces of the old vallum which formed the monastic boundary still survive.

The later church (built c 1825) in Clonown was dedicated to St Brigid and a well close by was dedicated to her also. Dean Kelly of St Peter's parish identified three 'patron' saints associated with Clonown. These were: St Brigid, St Colum (sometimes Colman) – feast-day 4th June, who was a priest of Clonown and St Ailill (sometimes thought to be one and the same as St Eamainn) whose feast day was celebrated on 1st July.

The road between Athlone and Clonown is very prone to flooding. The callows between Athlone and Clonown and between Clonown and Drumlosh are among the last habitats of the corncrake. In times past the communities in Clonown depended on the Shannon cot, a large flat bottomed boat, to get produce to and from the market in Athlone. The cots could carry a tonne and a half of turf or potatoes, they were also used to move hay from fields and when necessary to transport the coffins of loved ones across the Shannon to Clonmacnoise.

Clonown

Drum on the west side of Athlone is a great example of a local parish community which has come together to preserve its history and heritage. In the course of the past twenty years or so the Drum Heritage Group has among other works issued several important publications, restored the old monastic site and holy-well, recorded the mass paths and brought people along the ancient Pilgrim Road to Clonmacnoise as well as highlighting the works of Sean O'Neachtain, the seventeenth-century poet and writer who was born in Clonellan in the parish.

One of the earliest indicators we have for the settlement of the area around Athlone is the presence of a fine example of a megalithic tomb of the portal dolmen type, in the townland of Meehambee in Drum. This pre-Christian burial structure is to be found just off a bridal-path which links the townlands of Meehambee and Curraghaleen. It points to at least 2,000 years of habitation in this area.

Drum Old Church

Standing on an elevated site, the ancient monastic abbey at Drum dates from the 12th century and has several original Romanesque features. The importance of Druim Dreastann as a monastic site was recognised by St Brigid. The adjoining holy-well is dedicated to her, and the baptismal customs of this area are recorded in the *Book of Lecan,* where it describes the distribution of the 'Baptismal Penny' which was collected and divided three ways: one part to St Brigid's coarb at Brideswell, one part to Druim Dreastann and the third part to Cluain Eamhain (Clonown).

The Drum Heritage centre is well worth a visit and those wishing to trace their ancestral roots in Drum will be pleasantly surprised by the resources available here. While the town of Athlone continues to stretch out into the rural areas of south Roscommon, Drum still manages to retain a great deal of its rural charm. Glendeer Pet Farm is a great family attraction in the area and for those wishing to go further Derryglad Folk Museum, near Brideswell, offers a wonderful visitor experience with something for everyone.

Drum Farmyard

The Hill of Berries

Approaching the town from the Roscommon side, the Hill of Berries is one of the first great landmarks to herald your arrival in Athlone. It is a beautifully wooded hill which adds an extra dimension to the otherwise flat landscape. There are those who even consider that it marks the centre of Ireland. When viewed from the lake it is particularly impressive.

When I was a child I heard that this hill was planted, presumably as an eye-catcher, by a landed gentleman for his daughter. If I ever knew who that landed gentleman was I had long since forgotten it and I was amazed to realise that I couldn't find the history of the hill in any printed source. I remembered that some years ago I saw an early nineteenth century map of Lough Ree with a stand of trees, approximating to the present Hill of Berries, designated as 'Fort Arabella'. In an effort to tease out the history and to match the historical facts with the anecdotal evidence I examined details of landholders at the Berries in the eighteenth century.

My researches brought me back to the Jones family and in particular to one William Jones who served as an MP for Athlone. William was the second son and principal heir of Judge Oliver Jones who had also served as MP for Athlone. A barrister by profession William was the Recorder and Town Clerk for Athlone in the opening years of the eighteenth century. On his death in 1723 his extensive estate, which included properties in Athlone and south Roscommon, passed to his daughter and sole heiress, Arabella, the wife of John Reilly of the Berries.

It seems quite likely that when we look at the Hill of Berries now we are looking at William Jones's living monument to his daughter Arabella. Today a modern monument facing the road commemorates Toby Mannion who died as a result of a roadside encounter with the armed forces of the Free State in August 1923.

Athlone has been a garrison town since the late seventeenth century and it is claimed that officers of the garrison introduced the sport of golf to Athlone. The first introduction was probably quite informal but in 1892 the Athlone Garrison Golf Club was formed. The site of the first golf club was the abandoned Napoleonic fortifications on the Batteries. In 1895 under the guidance of Major R.A.G. Harrison the club began to develop and prosper. Soon the membership which had originally been confined to the military and police personnel spread to the professional and business people of Athlone.

Athlone Golf Club moved to a newly laid out course in Garnafailaigh in 1920, this move having been delayed by the intervention of World War I. In 1936 the club faced the decision whether to expand the course at Garnafailaigh or seek out a new course. It was decided to inspect land belong to Mr Gunning at Hodson Bay and it was agreed to rent the land at £65 per annum. In 1938 the move was made to Hodson Bay and this has been the home of Athlone Golf Club now for seventy years.

The course has been improved and altered over the years to take into account the competitive nature of the game. The old clubhouse was situated on the edge of Lough Ree but in the early 1970s the clubhouse moved to its present elevated site. The new clubhouse was designed by prominent club member and architect Mr Noel Heavey, and officially opened in August 1972.

Athlone Golf Club celebrated its centenary in 1992 with the publication of a history of the club written by a club member, and former Connacht Seniors' Champion, Tom Collins. That history is a much sought after today as a collectors item. After more than a century the game of golf is still one of the premier sports in this region with other fine golf courses to be found in Glasson, Mount Temple and Moate.

Athlone Golf Club, Hodson Bay

The controversial Irish playwright, Brendan Behan, once said that whenever a new political group came together for the first time and formed a committee the first item on the agenda was invariably the 'split'. The first Yacht Club in Athlone was formed in 1770 but it was sixty years before the 'split' came about. There is a suggestion in this case that the split was political. A small faction broke away and founded The Killinure Yacht Club in August 1831. A manuscript account of the rules of the new yacht club survived and was recorded by the late N.W. (Billy) English in his pioneering history of Lough Ree Yacht Club 1770-1970.

The first Commodore of The Killinure Yacht Club was Robert H. Temple a member of the landed gentry and the club-house was located on Temple Island. Other prominent members of the club included members of the Hodson family and other eminent people from the hinterland of Killinure including Major-General G. Murray of Killinure House. The rules of Killinure Yacht Club make amusing reading today.

Under Rule 3 we learn that each boat *'shall carry at her mast-head the distinguishing flag of the Club, viz. a 'white burgee' with the letters K.Y.C. in red…the Commodore and Vice-Commodore only to carry 'The Union Jack' at their peak'.*

Rule 5 states *'The members are always to appear on board their boats in the blue uniform…viz. blue jacket with appropriate buttons, waist-coat white cashmere with the club buttons, trousers blue, white or chequered, as the member may think proper to wear.'*

There were set fines for club members who attended meetings without their uniforms (2/6d) or for those who consumed more than 'one glass of grog' when the fleet was to return home after dinner the fine was five shillings. A 'mess' was provided for members but it was made clear, in Rule 11, that 'one servant only' was to be fed at the mess from each boat and two from the tender boat. Killinure Yacht Club survived until 1836 when it was disbanded and its members became reconciled with the parent body.

Temple Island

If we accept 1770 as the foundation date for Lough Ree Yacht Club that makes it the second oldest yacht club in the world. The first sixty years of the clubs existence have gone unrecorded but by 1831 the club, in the best Irish tradition, was the subject of a 'split'.

At this time there were two 'political groups' in the sailing fraternity – the Athlone Yacht Club and a short-lived breakaway group, the Killinure Yacht Club. The breakaway group had its own club-house on Temple Island in the inner lakes while Athlone Yacht Club had its club-house on Carberry Island. Five years later the Killinure Yacht Club was disbanded and the members had reunited with the parent club.

In 1895 the club reformed and took on its present title, Lough Ree Yacht Club. In 1914 it moved its club-house to Ballyglass where it still resides. Members of Lough Ree Yacht Club were to the fore in pressing for a standard design for an open centreboard sailing craft and so, in conjunction with other Shannon clubs, they established the Shannon One Design class. The Shannon One Design, designed by Morgan Giles, one of the leading British yacht designers of his day, was introduced in 1922. The sailing which was to be held on the last Wednesday in August that year was suspended because of the death of General Michael Collins in Cork. Today the Shannon One Design it is still the favourite craft among the most dedicated Shannon sailors.

Lough Ree Yacht Club has been around for almost 240 years and today it is a thriving yacht club with members participating in club, national and international competitions. It organises courses in sailing, aquatic expertise and boat management for a wide variety of people. Many young people get their first training in sailing at summer courses organised by Lough Ree Yacht Club – there can be very few sights as breathtaking as a yacht-race at Ballyglass. The earliest recorded regatta on Lough Ree was held from Monday, 28th July to Saturday, 2nd August 1731.

Marian Cross, Ballyglass

Lough Ree Yacht Club

Waterston demesne today consists of little more than the estate walls, the beautiful pigeon house, the ruins of the house, the remains of the walled garden and a lake complete with its folly. Waterston House was a great loss for south Westmeath which is not noted for its 'Big Houses'. Waterston was once described as *'one of the finest demesnes in Westmeath'* and this is not surprising when one realises that it was the work of Richard Castle (c 1690-1751).

Waterston, in the heart of Dillon country, had been the site of John Dillon's castle in the fifteenth century. During the Cromwellian confiscations the estate was granted to William Handcock and later his grandson married Elizabeth Temple, the heiress of Robert Temple of Ballyloughloe. The name Ballyloughloe was changed to Mount Temple to honour Elizabeth.

Her father, conscious that the Temple name was in danger of dying out, stipulated in his will that those who were to benefit from his estate should take the name Temple and thus the name Handcock-Temple came about. A century later the family was left once again with a sole heiress who married Lord Harris thus creating the name Temple-Harris. The Temple-Harris family occupied Waterston House until the estate was divided in 1923.

Waterston House was built in the 1740s to the design of Richard Castle, a Huguenot architect who came to Ireland to build Castle Hume in Fermanagh. He later worked with Lovett Pearce on the Parliament House and Pearce so admired his work that he recommended him to many parliamentarians as an architect for their houses.

The finest surviving feature of Waterston House is the pigeon house or dovecot designed by Castle. It stands on an elevated site inside the demesne walls and has a curious pinnacle appearance. Until modern farming methods provided root crops as cattle feed traditionally the majority of the livestock had to be slaughtered at the onset of winter. Thus there was always a shortage of meat during the winter months and so pigeons were reared to provide fresh meat for the table.

Kilkenny West

The Pigeon House, Waterston

The beautiful village of Glasson owes its existence to the nearby Waterston estate. Looking at the older elements of the village there is a great sense of uniformity reflecting the fact that it was built to house the workers on the estate. The buildings which have considerable architectural charm about them share a common eaves level and have good doors and windows.

In 1837 Samuel Lewis described Glasson as a village,

> 'containing thirty-three houses and 154 inhabitants. Here are two corn-mills, one of which is used for thickening frieze. There is a constabulary police station. Petty sessions for the barony are held on alternate Wednesdays. A patent for a market and fair exists but they are not held. There is a dispensary, and a penny post to Athlone and Ballymahon has been established.'

The village is known as 'The village of the roses' and this title obviously dates back to the nineteenth century at least. Mary Banim, a social commentator of the Victorian era who contributed articles to the Weekly Freeman which were subsequently published as *Here and there through Ireland* in 1891 observed:

The Three Jolly Pigeons, Goldsmith Country

> 'The houses are of picturesque build, and some are kept in the old style – smothered in roses and fuchsias; upon all are trained vines and climbing plants… The past landlord personally looked to the care of trees and flowers… indeed so much at heart had he the beauty of the cottages that it is said no inmate dare pluck a rose off his own house'.

Glasson has become synonymous with fine dining and tourism. It has the award-winning Glasson Village Restaurant and two pubs both of which serve fine food. The Wineport Restaurant and Hotel is another fine restaurant with an excellent reputation. This restaurant is at Portaneena (anglicised to Wineport), a name which recalls the landing of continental wines on the lakeshore in the early Christian period.

Near Glasson there is access to Lough Ree at Portaneena, Killinure and Portlick. Glasson itself is on the edge of the Goldsmith Country, Oliver Goldsmith, poet, novelist, playwright and essayist was reared at Lissoy parsonage 5kms north of the village.

Glasson Village

Westmeath is well known for its many lakes, rivers and waterways. It should come as no surprise to learn that it is also well served with golf clubs and that many of these enjoy picturesque lakeside settings. However, few can rival the idyllic setting of Glasson Golf and Country Club. It is located on the grounds of Killinure House which was built in the late eighteenth century by the Murray family. On an 1808 map of Lough Ree it is identified as 'Killynure' the property of 'Major Murray'. The house was extensively remodelled in the late nineteenth century and has a typically Victorian feel to it.

The lands at Killinure include some of the most beautifully wooded and rolling landscapes to be found on the eastern shores of Lough Ree. The proprietors Tom and Breda Reid, who previously farmed this land, have turned the grounds of Killinure House into a world-class golf club. The package includes a challenging and beautifully maintained golf course designed by Christy O'Connor Jnr. Together with a four star luxury hotel complex.

Bluebells in the woods

When the admiralty chart of Lough Ree was being surveyed in the 1830s it is said that the area around Killinure and Portlick received more than its share of attention. The survey was conducted by two naval officers, Commander Wolfe and Lieutenant Beechey. The younger one, Lt. R. B. Beechey, was courting Frideswide, the daughter of Robert Smyth of Portlick Castle at the time. The couple subsequently married and went to live in Dublin where R. B. Beechey went on to become one the greatest Irish marine painters of his generation.

In the nineteenth century there was a ferry service operating between Killinure and Coosan, the ferry route is recorded on the admiralty chart. The ferry served to bring workers from Athlone to and from a quarry in Killinure. In March 1845 the decrepit vessel sank resulting in the deaths of eight passengers – seven men and one woman. Only three passengers survived the tragedy.

Glasson Golf and Country Club

The Dillons were a Norman family who were granted lands in Kilkenny West by King John. They built castles and tower-houses throughout their new territory. But of about ten castles which they built, some have disappeared, others are in ruins and Portlick alone survives as an inhabited castle. It is basically a fourteenth century structure with a fine Tudor block and later Georgian and Victorian additions.

Apart from short periods when Portlick was vacant it has been in continuous occupation since Norman times. The Dillons lived at Portlick until the late 17th century. Throughout their history many of the Dillons remained steadfast Catholics. They took the Irish side in the rebellion of 1641 and consequently suffered heavy losses during the Cromwellian settlements. They also supported the Jacobite cause and many of them later fled to Europe with the Wild Geese where they distinguished themselves in continental armies.

Portlick and its lands were granted to Thomas Keightly in 1696 but by 1703 it had been acquired by Rev Robert Smyth. The Smyths occupied the Castle until 1956. It has changed hands several times since and in recent years has operated as a private hotel or guest-house.

From the picnic area at Portlick there is a right of way to the foreshore and to a woodland walk of almost a mile to the point at Whinning. The ruined house at Whinning was another Smyth residence which was occupied in the 1860s. The woods at Portlick are famed for their bluebells. The walk offers an oasis of peace and tranquillity and can be a rewarding experience for the naturalist at any time.

Nearby there is a beautiful chalet development at Clonakilla Point. The complex has a reconstructed crannog, a number of chalets and a centre which is ideal for courses or meetings. Even for those living in Athlone it provides a quiet retreat from the pressures of daily life. It is an ideal base for fishing or boating holiday breaks.

Benown Church

Portlick Walk

John Keegan Casey, the quintessential Midlander, was born in Westmeath in 1846. He was one of the great poets of the Fenian period and is best remembered for his rousing ballad *The Rising of the Moon*.

As surely as the Avon was the river of William Shakespeare, John Keegan Casey's river was the Inny. How he loved its easy movement, the bridges and the mills, the bird life and the fish. He spent his happiest hours either boating on Lough Ree or lazing on the banks of the Inny with a pencil and paper at the ready. One quatrain from his poem *The Inny – A Contrast* captures the poet's feeling for the river.

> 'No ship cast anchor on its soft bright tide
> But all was silence by its flowery brink
> Save when a dreamer sought its quiet side
> And there on God's bright beauty sat to think'

John Keegan Casey captured the midland landscape better than most. He celebrated the rivers and streams, the villages and hamlets, the townlands and the rolling hills. One of the most beautiful of all his poems, which celebrates the countryside, is the evocative lyric poem *Among the Flowers*.

> 'In leafy Tang the wild birds sang -
> The brown light lay on Derry's heather;
> But years have pass'd since we the last
> Sat courting in the summer weather:
> The tender light of stars at night,
> That soothes the wanderer so weary,
> Could only show the silvery glow
> That lit your glance, my darling Mary!'

John Keegan Casey died in Dublin on 17th March, 1870 and contemporary accounts suggest that 50,000 people marched in the funeral procession with over 100,000 looking on.

Mill on the Inny

Moydrum Castle was a gentleman's residence of the early 19th century built in the Gothic Revival style. It was the seat of the first Baron Castlemaine, William Handcock. He belonged to a family which had been granted extensive lands under the Cromwellian Plantations. The first of these Handcocks, also William, was granted over 7,000 acres near Athlone and later added to his estate. In 1680 he was granted a royal patent to build a manor house at Twyford.

Sir Jonah Barrington writes,

> *'Will. Handcock an extraordinary instance; he made and sang songs against the Union in 1799 at a public dinner of the opposition, and made and sang songs for it in 1800. He got a peerage.'*

It was also the opinion of the Westmeath historian, John Charles Lyons, that William who was MP for Athlone and who had once been so outspoken against the Act of Union, eventually succumbed to the promise of a title and voted in favour of it.

William Handcock received his title in 1812 and quickly set about having a new seat built to reflect his new-found status. In employing the services of the architect Sir Richard Morrison to design his 'castle', he was making a statement that he had arrived. Here, for over a century, he and his successors entertained members of the nobility and royalty who visited Athlone. The house survived until 1921 when it was maliciously burned in retaliation for the burning of three houses in Coosan by Crown forces.

When the IRA forces approached Moydrum in the early hours of the morning they learned that Lord Castlemaine was away on business. They gave his wife and daughters time to dress and leave. Lady Castlemaine requested an extension of time to allow them to remove some family silver and other heirlooms. This was granted and according to local lore chairs were brought on to the lawn for the ladies to sit and watch as their home burned to the ground.

The ghostly ruin of Moydrum is perhaps most famous today because it appeared on the album cover of U2's *Unforgettable Fire*.

Moydrum Bog

A short spin from Athlone will bring you to the village of Ballinahowen, which is located on the Westmeath-Offaly border, about mid-way between Athlone and Clonmacnoise. In recent years the environs of the village have been greatly enhanced by a local 'Tidy Towns' committee.

Ballinahowen is within easy reach of an exciting array of attractions and no matter where your interests lie there will be a choice of short drives to find places of interest. Within the village, in the old schoolhouse, is the Celtic Roots Studio. Celtic Roots was established in the early 1990s to give employment to local men who had previously worked with Bord na Mona. Initially a small cohort of apprentice craftsmen was trained by Michael Casey, the noted bog-wood sculptor. They now produce a varied and affordable range of art-works made from ancient oak, yew and elm which has been salvaged from the midland bogs. A visit to this studio is highly recommended.

For bog lovers there are several attractions near Ballinahowen: Mongan Bog, the beautiful Boora Parklands and the Clonmacnoise and West Offaly Railway at Blackwater Bog to name but a few. Those who have had their eyes opened by the beauty of the work of Celtic Roots Studio might like to visit Pullagh Church with its bog-wood features by Michael Casey. Banagher, famous for its literary connections with both Anthony Trollope and the Brontes, is a picturesque town on the Shannon. Shannonbridge with its Napoleonic fortification and Killeen's Bar which is noted for its hospitality, is always worth a visit. Those in search of history and archaeology could be lured by the attractions of the Clonfinlough Stone and/or St Manchan's Shrine which is housed in Boher Church. The Clonfinlough Stone, a large carved rock 3km east of Clonmacnoise was carved during the Bronze Age. St Manchan's Shrine is a twelfth century reliquary in bronze and enamel. It has been exhibited both nationally and internationally and is a stunning example from the golden age of Irish metalwork. There are also some wonderful public sculptures to be found in this general area.

Farmhouse at Ballinahowen

The best way to visit Clonmacnoise is to arrive there by water – and the Viking boat from Athlone is an ideal vessel on which to travel. Today Clonmacnoise welcomes over 100,000 visitors per annum. A millennium ago, while certain continental visitors were welcomed and became part of the great city of learning, the sight of an approaching Viking longboat was perhaps the most dreaded sight that a watchman could report.

The journey downstream is through the Shannon callows – an area of great ecological interest. This area, which is largely unspoilt, retains the same characteristics which the monks would have observed during the Golden Age of Clonmacnoise. The callows is the term applied to the land in the flood-plain of the river which is submerged in winter by the rich, silt-laden floodwater and which, when it dries out in the summer, provides excellent hay-making and grazing facilities.

Poppies

The Heritage Service at Clonmacnoise is excellent. The visitor centre is practical, unobtrusive and attractive. The art work including the fine metalwork by Dan Edwards and the sculpture of 'The Pilgrim' by Jackie McKenna are wonderful examples of modern Irish craftsmanship and deserve to be shown side by side with some of the finest examples of the stone-mason's art.

There are many attractions at Clonmacnoise: the cathedral, the round towers and high-crosses and the early-Christian grave slabs. However for me part of the Clonmacnoise experience has to be reading the headstones in both the old and new cemeteries and I never consider a visit to Clonmacnoise complete without a visit to the beautiful Romanesque nuns' chapel. Clonmacnoise has something to offer everyone – whether it's the sheer tranquillity of the place, the beautiful view of the meandering Shannon in summer or the sighting of a charm of goldfinches in the hedgerow.

The many excavations which have taken place at Clonmacnoise in recent years have added greatly to our knowledge of life in this ancient monastic community. Now there is an abundance of useful literature on Clonmacnoise which will help to satisfy even the most enthusiastic visitors.

Temple Finghin and Round Tower, Clonmacnoise

The monastic site of Clonmacnoise was one of the great university 'cities' of Europe until its decline in the thirteenth century. Of all the surviving features one of the most appealing is the Nuns' Church which stands about a quarter of a mile from the main site, adjoining the ancient Pilgrim's Way. Here in a field, on the side of a narrow road, are the remains of a beautiful Romanesque church which was restored in the 1860s by the Kilkenny Archaeological Society.

In 1026 there was mention of a paved way being constructed from the church in the abbess's garden or enclosure to the mound of the three crosses, presumably within the monastic enclosure itself. Sixty years later this early church was burned but rudimentary remains of it survive near the present church. The rebuilding of the Nuns' church, in its present form, is credited to Dervogilla, the wife of Tigernan O'Rourke, in the year 1167.

In 1152 at the height of territorial disputes between provincial kings, the king of Leinster and the king of the Connacht gained the upper hand against the king of Meath. They then targeted the kingdom of Breffni. They defeated Tigernan O'Rourke in battle and took a 'great spoil' which included his wife Dervogilla (then aged forty-four) who was abducted by Dermot McMurrogh, king of Leinster during the raid.

According to the *Annals of Clonmacnoise,*

'Dermot McMurrogh king of Leinster tooke the lady Dervorgill, daughter of the said Morrogh O'Melaghlin, and wife of Tyernan O'Royrck, with her cattle with him, and kept her for a long space to satisfie his insatiable, carnall and adulterous lust.'

Today as it stands in tranquillity there is little to suggest the sordid details of Dervogilla's connection with Clonmacnoise. She is also associated with another monastic site as she was a benefactor of the great Cistercian abbey of Mellifont, in County Louth. Dervogilla, wife of Tigernan O'Rourke and mistress of Dermot McMurrogh, retired to Mellifont in 1186 and died there seven years later at the age of 85.

The Nuns' Church, Clonmacnoise

When I was a child returning from holidays or outings of any sort there were only a few landmarks which heralded our return to Athlone. The first en-route from Dublin was always the twin masts at the Moydrum transmitter and approaching from the west the twin spires of SS Peter & Paul's church served a similar function. Later from the west the great bulk of the Battery Heights complex was the dominant landmark but that is all now changed.

I find myself constantly fascinated by the evolving skyline of Athlone as seen from the various approaches to the town. The twin masts of Moydrum are still an early signal of the approach to Athlone from the east. However, the massive telephone mast at Roslevin is perhaps the most dominant feature. When the idea of an eleven story hotel complex as part of the Gallico Town Centre development was first mooted there were those who felt it would dominate the skyline. In reality it fits in quite snugly with only a few stories peeping above the parapet.

The approach to suburban Athlone now starts at the Creggan roundabout in the east and ends around Summerhill in the west. Looking across at the Athlone skyline from the Clonown Road recently I was struck by the extent and bulk of our built environment. Some of the old landmarks are still there but they are no longer quite as obvious. Athlone has surely expanded more in the past two decades than in did in the previous century.

However, to really appreciate the expanding nature of Athlone it is only necessary to approach it from any direction at night. To my mind the night-lights of Athlone now are reminiscent of the approach to Dublin in the 1960s. Who knows what the dominant features will be in a century's time? I'm sure that some of those features that we know and love will still be vying for attention and the many spires of Athlone will still hold pride of place on the ever evolving skyline.

Athlone Skyline from Clonown

Athlone through the Ages

Given its strategic location we must assume that this crossing point of the Shannon has been of importance since time immemorial. A catalogue of stray archaeological finds from the river-bed at Athlone, some of which were discovered during the Shannon navigation works of the 1840s and others more recently by members of Athlone Sub-Aqua Club, army divers and others, confirm the importance of this crossing point in both the Neolithic and Bronze ages. A further clue to the Neolithic settlement in the area is provided by the survival of a fine portal dolmen in Mihanboy, in the parish of Drum, and by a putative passage-grave in Clonbrusk townland.

The ford itself was formed after the last Ice Age when the great Esker Riada and other minor eskers were being laid down. These eskers formed a band of sand and gravel ridges stretching across the island in an east-west alignment. As the esker crossed the mighty Shannon it left a great deal of glacial deposits in the bed of the river. These glacial deposits formed a natural ford with shallows and rapids rendering the middle Shannon unnavigable. It was not until the 1840s that these deposits from the Ice Age were cleared from the bed of the river opening up the Shannon to the movement of larger craft.

In terms of the Early Christian period tradition claims that St Patrick himself passed this way in the fifth century. St Ciaran founded two important monasteries in this area (one at Hare Island on Lough Ree and the other down river at Clonmacnoise). The presence of a host of Early Christian settlements on the islands of Lough Ree and monastic sites at Kilkenny-West, Clonown and Drum all point towards the significance of Athlone at this time. The discovery of a small number of elaborate Early Christian grave-slabs of the Clonmacnoise type in the Abbey Graveyard in Athlone suggests the possibility of a previously unrecorded monastic settlement at Athlone.

A Viking Presence

There were two distinct periods of Viking activity on Lough Ree north of Athlone. In the ninth century, attracted by the wealth of the monasteries on Lough Ree, the Vikings arrived and were present on the lake between 832 and 845. Turgesius, a fearless warrior, was one of the leaders of a strong Viking fleet. At Clonmacnoise he set up his wife, Ota, as a pagan goddess on the altar from where she delivered oracles. He moved his fleet northwards obviously carrying the longships on their shoulders through the rapids at Athlone before setting sail on Lough Ree. According to tradition Turgesius set up a Viking base on Lough Ree, possibly at Rindoon, from where he could launch forays both to the east and west. Turgesius was captured by the High-King Malachy on Lough Ennel in 845 and put to death. His death ended this first bout of Viking activity on the lake.

In 923 another Viking king, Tamar MacAilche, who had made his way from Limerick to Lough Ree *'plundered all the islands of the lake and carried off great spoil, between gold, silver and other treasures'*. Later, in 936, Olafr Cenncairech (Olaf scabby-head) king of Limerick moved his fleet overland from the Erne to Lough Ree. The following year Olafr Gothfrithsson, king of Dublin, attacked his ships and took him and his followers to Dublin as prisoners. This was a crucial victory for Olafr Gothfrithsson who became the overlord of all the Norse towns in Ireland.

In 1802 a huge Viking gold hoard was found on Hare Island. It contained *'ten gold bracelets, a number of silver anklets, and some ingots of silver'*. They were sold in Dublin for £700 but later brought to London where they were consigned to the melting pot. A contemporary estimate put the intrinsic value of the hoard at *'nearly a thousand guineas'*.

Some years ago archaeologists investigated the site of a possible Viking 'longport' and boat-shed near Ballykeeran. The dig was inconclusive, as no stray Viking finds were made, but the earthworks which attracted the investigation were very convincing and the archaeologist concerned later stated that he still believed that the site may well have been an abandoned 'longport' which was developed but never used due to the sudden disappearance of the Vikings from Lough Ree.

Anglo-Norman Settlement

While it is widely acknowledged that the modern town of Athlone has Anglo-Norman origins, and the Normans certainly influenced the growth of the settlement, some of the credit must surely be given to the O'Conors of Connaught. In looking at the evidence of the various Irish annals we know that by the ninth century, at least, Athlone was one of the most notable Irish fording places. By the year 1000 a causeway had been constructed for Mael Sechnaill II, High-King of Ireland and Cathal O'Conor, King of Connaught. This causeway played a role in impeding the progress of the marauding fleet of Brian Boru, King of Munster. The surrender of the Munster fleet in 1087 enabled the rise to power of the O'Conors in Connaught.

The Arrival of the Cluniac Monks.

According to tradition it was King Turlough O'Conor, who introduced the Cluniac monks to Athlone c1150. They were granted extensive lands on the west bank of the Shannon, a portion of which was later confiscated for the building of Athlone Castle. The Cluniac monks were a reformed Benedictine order and the priory at Athlone was the only house of the order in Ireland.

The Cluniac house was known as the Priory of SS Peter & Paul or de Innocentia. The monks received valuable grants of eel fisheries for which they paid the Crown an annual rent. In 1290 they were compensated with forty shillings in silver because of losses sustained in their fisheries due to pollution from the king's mills.

The Cluniac priory, in common with other Irish monasteries, had shown a general decline in standards prior to the Reformation. It survived until the dissolution of the monasteries when its property was annexed to that of the Castle.

The First Bridge of Athlone.

According to the *Annals of the Four Masters* a bridge was built at Athlone by Turlough O'Conor, King of Connaught and High-King of Ireland in 1120. This was clearly a wooden structure as the annals record the building and destruction of at least five more bridges over the next forty years. As they were built each successive bridge was destroyed by the marauding armies of Meath men. Turlough O'Conor was also responsible for the building of the first castle at Athlone in 1129. Like the bridges it too was evidently made of timber as it perished when hit by a thunderbolt in 1131. Undaunted O'Conor rebuilt it but no sooner was it completed than it was destroyed once again by the Mael-Sechlainns, Kings of Meath. And so the story goes with bridges and castles being rebuilt by the O'Conors and destroyed by the Mael-Sechlainns throughout this turbulent century. This early 'castle' may have stood where the present Athlone Castle now stands as there is evidence to suggest that it is built on top of an ancient motte.

The Arrival of the Normans.

John de Grey, Bishop of Norwich may have used an existing motte as a site for the first stone castle of Athlone in 1210. He was King John's Irish Justiciar and was responsible for the building of the first stone bridge over the Shannon at Athlone a few years earlier. We know very little about that bridge, which was destroyed by Aodh O'Conor in 1271 and if rebuilt, survived for less than fifty years. It was eventually replaced with a ferry in the early fourteenth century and the next major fording exercise was carried out during the reign of Queen Elizabeth in 1566-67 when a new stone bridge was built.

By the thirteenth century a town was beginning to emerge at Athlone with the nucleus of settlement centred around the Castle on the west bank. On the east bank the O'Breens of Brawney, an indigenous Gaelic family, had their castles at Coosan and Garrycastle and were patrons of church on the site of the present St Mary's Church of Ireland. By 1239 the Franciscans had arrived in Athlone and set up a friary at a site unknown to us.

By now the town had begun to develop both east and west of the Shannon. The linear lay-out of Church Street, Dublingate Street and Mardyke Street are typical of the street-pattern of an Anglo-Norman town. To the west the twin benefits of relative security and employment opportunities presented by the proximity of the Castle encouraged settlement and a series of small streets began to radiate out from it. The next major development of Athlone was the building of the town walls in 1251.

Town Walls

In medieval times the Crown encouraged the building of town walls to protect the inhabitants of all important settlements. From a report in the official *Calendar of Documents Relating to Ireland* of 1251 we can see that the authorities in Athlone applied for and received a murage grant (i.e. a grant to build a wall) but sadly we do not know the nature or extent of this wall. Indeed apart from a few references to a wall in a state of disrepair we could be tempted to assume that the grant was paid but that the wall was never built. Whatever type of wall was built it was clearly inadequate for the purposes for which it was intended.

In the Annals of Clonmacnoise we read that in 1316,

> *ffelym O'Conor…prepared an army with whome hee went to banish the English of Conaught. Immediately burnt the towne of Athlone, killed Stephen Dexeter therin, Miles Cogan, William Prendergrasse, & John Stanton, knights & alsoe William Lawless, with a great slaughter of their people.'*

This was a devastating blow to the fledgling town which heralded the decline of the Norman settlement here and the start of hostilities between the Dillons of Kilkenny-West and the O'Kellys of Hy-many for the control of the Athlone castle.

Features of the Early Town

Medieval Athlone probably consisted of the Castle with some houses, shops and inns built in the vicinity to service the needs of the officials stationed there. On the west bank of the river stood the Cluniac monastery with its eel weirs and fisheries and on the east bank a Franciscan friary possibly located outside the town walls. A small parish church, founded by the O'Breens c1100, was most likely situated on the site of the present Church of Ireland and the Bawn area, just inside the town-wall, was a safe enclosure for the cattle of the inhabitants.

The destruction of Athlone in 1316 certainly halted the growth of this urban centre. Those who remained were, most likely, the native Irish while the Anglo-Normans moved on to Rindoon and Roscommon where they enjoyed the protection of the royal castles. It seems remarkable to us today that the abandoned walled-town of Rindoon, located near the village of Lecarrow, on a promontory in Lough Ree was once a more important settlement than Athlone. However the situation was later to turn full circle with the revival of Athlone and the abandonment of Rindoon.

The first real sign of improvement in Athlone was the recovery of the Castle for the crown in 1537. Prior to this the Castle had changed hands several times between the Dillons and the O'Kellys. The new expression of interest by the Crown was recognition once again of the strategic importance of Athlone.

The Castle and the Presidency of Connaught

As soon as the Castle was in Crown control the building was repaired and strengthened. By 1547 a small permanent garrison was stationed here under the command of Sir William Brabazon, the Vice-Treasurer of the Dublin administration who had been appointed as Governor of Athlone Castle. The next few Vice-Treasurers enjoyed the status of Governor of the Castle under their terms of office. In 1569 Sir Edward Fitton was appointed President of Connaught and given Athlone Castle as his seat of power.

The Presidency of Connaught was established in 1569 to hasten the process of bringing the province under English law. The administration consisted of a president and a council. The president enjoyed wide powers within the province including responsibility for civil, criminal and ecclesiastical matters; he also commanded all military forces and appointed his own officials.

One of those who held the prestigious office was Sir Nicholas Malby who did much to pacify Connaught and who was responsible for extensive remodelling of Roscommon Castle. Other well known presidents of Connaught were the ferocious

Richard Bingham and Sir Conyers Clifford who was defeated and killed by Red Hugh O'Donnell at the battle of the Curlews in 1599.

Writing of Roscommon Castle, the late Tim Cronin wrote:

'You can visualise the strange cavalcade that entered through its multi-storied gate-house; the old aristocratic Sidney; the bungling Fitton; those dashing swordsmen Malby and Conyers Clifford; the calculating and complaining Fitwilliam with a mulish Bingham lashing out at friend and foe alike. Falstaff would indeed have been at home in this company…'

This description could equally apply to Athlone Castle.

The Suppression of the monasteries

King Henry VIII was proclaimed head of the Church in Ireland in 1536 and the following year a bill was passed through parliament to suppress the monasteries in this country. The Franciscans in Athlone seem to have gone quietly into hiding leaving the valuables of their Friary to some trustworthy friends. By 1588 their property was leased to John Bryan but nine years later the Friary was almost completely destroyed by the military forces.

The Cluniacs, on the West bank survived there until after Sir William Brabazon took over as constable of Athlone Castle. The monastic property was joined to that of the Castle giving the Crown a very valuable property in Athlone. This enlarged holding was in the possession of the Irish vice-treasurers until 1569 when it became the property of the president of Connaught. In 1572 the sons of the Earl of Clanricard attacked Athlone and burned the old church. The storekeeper, John Crofton reported that his *'malt, biscuit, and beer, and all his brewing and baking vessels'* had been consumed in the fire.

The Gate-houses

Apart from the destruction of some parts of the town the sixteenth century witnessed some significant developments also. Two major gate-houses to guard the entrances to Athlone from the east were built at that time. These were the East-Gate (or Dublin Gate) and the Northgate. In a contemporary source the East-Gate is described as a 'castle' which was built by, and leased to, Edmund O Fallon in 1578-79. The Northgate was a rectangular gate-house, sometimes referred to as a castle and it too was built at this time. Several images of the Northgate exist as it survived until the 1840s but there are no known images of the Dublin Gate.

The Elizabethan Bridge

The greatest legacy of Elizabethan times to the town of Athlone was, undoubtedly, the building of a stone bridge in 1566. The bridge was built at the request of the Lord Deputy, Sir Henry Sidney and the architect was Sir Peter Lewis. The building of this bridge was a major feat of engineering. We are told that it was completed within a year. The bridge itself was 360 feet long and 14 feet wide. It consisted of ten stone arches supported on piers built on stones thrown into the river and held in position by wooden piles. There were a number of mills constructed on the bridge to take advantage of the water-power. This bridge ran behind the modern Ritz Cinema site across the river from Bridge Street to Main Street. It was to serve Athlone for over 300 years and become a major asset to the development of the town. It also played a pivotal role in the famous sieges of Athlone in 1690 and 1691. It was, however, built for foot-passage and the occasional tumbrel or rustic cart and by the mid-nineteenth century had become an obstacle to traffic in the town. Weld's *Statistical Survey of County Roscommon* published in 1832 described it as *'not merely a discredit to the town alone but a positive stigma upon the nation'*.

Athlone in the Seventeenth Century

The seventeenth century was a crucial century in the history of the town. Thanks to the early researches Dr G.T. Stokes and the recent researches of Dr Harman Murtagh we have a very comprehensive account of life in Athlone in the seventeenth century. Both of these eminent historians were born in Athlone.

The following information has been gleaned from an important article by Stokes called *Athlone in the Seventeenth Century* which was published in the *Journal of the Royal Society of Antiquaries* in 1890-91. When George T. Stokes was writing in 1890 he had the advantage of having strong local connections as well as easy access to both local and national archives. It is not surprising therefore that he was the first to record several interesting and important facts relating to Athlone. In earlier histories it had been commonly assumed that the Charter granted to Athlone in 1606 was the first charter to be granted to the town. Dr Stokes unearthed evidence of an Elizabethan charter, granted through the Earl of Essex in 1599.

Stokes captures for us the state of Athlone in 1599:

> *'... Athlone was simply a military colony or settlement, where the Constable or Governor of the Castle reigned supreme. Athlone was rapidly growing, however and becoming a commercial centre. The 'new bridge' as it was then called - old, inconvenient, narrow, as it was considered when swept away, fifty years ago - the 'new bridge', built by Sir Henry Sidney in 1566, was a great*

improvement on the wretched temporary structure which had preceded it; and the people of Athlone wished to enjoy the municipal government which had made many of the towns of Ireland rich and flourishing. So they applied to Queen Elizabeth for a charter of incorporation…'

Since Stokes' time the evidence points to the fact that Athlone was, most likely, granted an Anglo-Norman charter in the early thirteenth century. However no documentary evidence survives to substantiate this claim but references contained in the *Calendar of Documents Relating to Ireland 1171-1251* and *1285-92* and cited by Dr Harman Murtagh in his *Historic Towns Atlas of Athlone* confirm this theory.

Dr Stokes examined an early document, a Cromwellian survey, which bore the title *Lands and Tenements of Athlone in the year 1641, and also of all the dowries, fortunes, mortgages, church lands etc.* This survey detailed all the property and houses on the Leinster side of Athlone, *'stating all the mortgages upon them down to the very dowries given and received with the wives and daughters of the townsmen'*. Viscount Wilmot, as President of Connacht, granted good-titles to property holders in Athlone between 1618 and 1622 which authorised the rebuilding of these houses *'in the English manner'*, that is of slate and stone. The survey of 1641 confirms that many of the houses from Custume Place to Mardyke Street appear to have been built between 1620 and 1650.

THE SIEGES OF ATHLONE

Anyone wishing to learn all about the famous Sieges of Athlone, the most dramatic events in the history of Athlone, should read Dr Harman Murtagh's *Athlone: history and settlement to 1800*. Dr Murtagh is the greatest authority on the early history of Athlone and an acknowledged expert on the Williamite and Jacobite wars in Ireland.

The first assault on Athlone came in 1690 after the defeat of the Irish at the Boyne. General Douglas, leading a substantial force consisting mostly of Ulster regiments, was the Williamite commander. His troops possibly numbered 10,000 but certainly no less than 7,500. When he arrived at Athlone he was confident that he would conquer the town for King William within twenty four hours. His confidence was misplaced because he had not reckoned on the spirited defence of Athlone by Colonel Richard Grace. Grace, who was at that time over seventy years of age, a veteran of the Confederate War and Governor of Athlone, refused to surrender. After a week the Williamite army retreated.

In 1691 determined to capture Athlone, the Williamites returned with their full army of almost 25,000 men. The army was under the command of a Dutch general, Godard de Ginkle. The Jacobite forces were under the command of a French general, the Marquis de St. Ruth. The Williamites breached the town wall and captured the Leinster town. The Jacobites in a desperate attempt to keep the enemy at bay, broke down several arches of the bridge and the Williamites quickly attempted to repair them. In an act of unspeakable bravery a sergeant of dragoons named Custume lead his men onto the bridge to dislodge the Williamite repair work, this they did before meeting their death at the hands of enemy fire.

Ironically the capture of Athlone came when the Williamites discovered the ford that gave Athlone its name and in a surprise attack dislodged the Jacobites and took the castle by storm resulting in wholesale carnage and slaughter. For his services to King Billy, but certainly not to Athlone, Ginkle was given the title Earl of Athlone.

The Eighteenth Century

The century following the Siege was generally a quiet period in the history of the town. Obviously a great deal of rebuilding of the castle and the houses of the town took place and the military barracks expanded and became an important part of life in Athlone.

Commercial life slowly recovered and a number of inns became established including The Three Blackamoor Heads. It was Mark Begg, the proprietor of 'The Three Blacks' who established the first stage-coach service between Athlone and Dublin in the mid-eighteenth century. Another attempt to improve communications was the cutting of Athlone Canal in 1757 as part of the solution to the navigation problems at Athlone.

Athlone also became the centre of a thriving felt hat manufacturing trade. The hatters were to be found in Baylough and also in close proximity to the Shannon near the present AIB Bank. The small laneway, in front of the bank, leading to the river is called Hatter's Lane as was a cross-lane linking it to Malthouse Lane. The industry survived until the nineteenth century but was at the height of its fame in the time of Dean Swift who once wrote *'Those who are born in this country will think themselves abundantly happy when they can afford an Athlone hat'*. Among those who wore Athlone hats were the pensioners in the Royal Hospital in Kilmainham.

Inhabitants of Athlone obviously still found plenty of time for recreation as is evidenced by the presence of a horse-racing course at Monksland from 1731 and the founding of a yacht club in 1770.

Athlone through the Ages

The Nineteenth Century

For any one who wishes to learn more about Athlone in the nineteenth century I would recommend John Burkes *Athlone in the Victorian era* which gives great insights into the state of Athlone and the lives of the inhabitants during this great period of growth and consolidation.

The Victorian era saw a great deal of important infrastructural changes in Athlone. Indeed it would be true to say that the town took on its present shape at that time. There were so many important developments that it is difficult to know where to start. One of the great works which surely helped to put Athlone on the map was the Shannon navigation works of the 1840s. These works endowed the town with a river which now had defined banks, a spacious lock, a weir wall and a new bridge. Prior to this the state of the river was contributing to the spread of disease with stagnant pools and marshy banks providing a breeding ground for infection. The absence of impediments in the river bed and the building of a lock made the stretch of river at Athlone fully navigable. The building of a new bridge replaced one which was narrow and totally unsuitable so the new bridge contributed to a new sense of prosperity in the town.

The Coming of the Railway

The mid-nineteenth century also saw the arrival of the railway in Athlone. Suddenly it was possible to visit Dublin on business and arrive home the same day. A new and exciting railway bridge spanned the Shannon within sight of the town bridge and a new railway station was built. The cutting of the railway and the ancillary works gave massive employment in Athlone and the first systematic attempt to bring visitors into Athlone was made by offering a package of a day trip to Athlone to include a steamer trip on Lough Ree. The railway companies produced guide books and suddenly 'visitor attractions' had to be found or created. A number of tourist related stories emerged then which seem to have gone unrecorded prior to this. The burial place of Richard Grace was identified by the presence of a crude cross on the boundary wall of St Mary's Church of Ireland; a house in Custume Place was identified as the house occupied by Ginkle in 1691 and later by the Duke of Wellington when he was a young subaltern in Athlone; a field in the military barracks was said to have been the burial ground of Wellington's horse which he rode at Waterloo. These and other stories entered the canon of stories about Athlone.

It was believed that one of the great advantages of the railway would be that rail transport would be considerably cheaper than the conventional transport costs of the day. Initially this may have been the case but rising transport charges gave great cause for concern to the major industrialists in Athlone. Brewing and distilling were among the largest industrial concerns in the early nineteenth century but later the greatest employment prospects in Athlone were in Athlone Woollen Mills and in the large Saw Mills on the docks. Athlone had a noteworthy furniture manufacturing industry and Athlone chairs were sold all over Ireland.

The Twentieth Century

In the early years of the twentieth century Victoria Barracks, Athlone was still a recruiting ground for the British Army. For generations Athlone men had joined the army here to serve in foreign wars including the Crimean and Boer wars. Hordes of young men from Athlone joined the army and saw service in the First World War and some of these who returned to Athlone after the war were among the first officers of the Free State Army.

The hand-over of the Castle and Barracks from the British in 1922 was a red letter day in Athlone. The Barracks was handed over to Commandant General Sean MacEoin and the name was quickly changed from Victoria Barracks to Custume Barracks. When the army arrived in the Castle to raise the tricolour it was discovered that there was no flag pole. Local photographer, G. V. Simmons, saved the day when he presented the mast of his yacht as a temporary flag-pole.

Athlone Woollen Mills, employing up to 500 hands, was one of the largest employers in Athlone. The accidental burning of the Mills in 1940 was a most devastating blow to the town. The Woollen Mills re-opened after the fire but never regained the lost ground. When the Mills eventually closed the premises were taken over and became Athlone Apparel Co. Ltd.

The next largest employer was Gentex (General Textiles), the cotton factory which opened in the 1930s and for fifty years produced high quality textiles including the celebrated Constellation bed-linen. Following its closure in 1984, Athlone became dependent on a greater diversity of industries – today companies such as Elan, Mallinckrodt Medical, L. M. Erricsson, Athlone Extrusions and Nexans (Ireland) are among the most established names.

Athlone in the New Millennium

Athlone has witnessed a great growth in the hospitality sector with major new hotels and conference facilities being built in recent years. The most recent of these is the eleven-storey Athlone Sheraton Hotel which is part of the new Town Centre development. While Athlone is not a major tourism destination the town continues to attract many tourists who are attracted to the Shannon, and the recent development and extension of marina facilities is to be welcomed. Shopping is catered for throughout the town and there are dedicated shopping centres at Irishtown, Golden Island and Athlone Town Centre.

The building of a new Civic Centre in 2004, to the design of Keith Williams, architect, has endowed Athlone with a major modern building which shows a great confidence in the future of Athlone. Included in the Civic Centre which boasts state of the art facilities are offices for Athlone Town Council and Westmeath County Council, a new Council Chamber and The Aidan Heavey Public Library. The Aidan Heavey Library also houses the prestigious Aidan Heavey Collection – an Irish interest, closed-access collection, which attracts scholars to Athlone because of the range of unique and rare items which it contains.

The adjacent Town Centre development completed in 2007 is a further indication of the confidence of the developers in the future of Athlone. Here, as with a new development in Connaught Street, a combination of retail units and residential units helps to bring life back into the town centre.

A Few Famous Athlonians

Since the time of Luan himself there must have been many famous, or perhaps notorious, Athlonians. Unfortunately the names of many of them have been lost over the centuries. We know so little about the 'famous' Sergeant Custume that it is almost a source of embarrassment to us. His name has been preserved for posterity in only one original source. Or has it? We don't even know his Christian name, we don't know where he was from – was he a local? We don't even know his surname for certain – no one that I have met has ever known someone called Custume so perhaps the historian of the day got it wrong. We do know that he was a 'Sergeant of Dragoons in Maxwell's regiment' and we do know that the army barracks in Athlone is named in his honour and we do know of his brave deeds.

In this section I will give brief pen-pictures of some Athlone natives who have made their mark nationally or internationally. For obvious reasons I will not be including the living in this 'Hall of Fame'. It would be foolish of me to include sports-people or politicians – both of these categories could fill a book in their own right. Athlone has produced several sport stars that have represented Ireland including Olympians in both soccer and basketball. We have also produced several distinguished golfers and tennis players and in more recent times we have had great success in sailing, swimming and a host of other sports.

In terms of politicians we had MPs returned for the Borough of Athlone including the notorious Judge Keogh and several members of both the St George and Handcock families. In terms of Irish politics our first home-grown TD was Harry Broderick of the Labour Party and since we have had Patrick Cooney who has served in the Dail, the Seanad and the European Parliament, and members of the Lenihan dynasty – including Brian Lenihan who held several ministerial posts and served as Tánaiste, his sister Mary O'Rourke also held several ministerial roles and high office in the Seanad and their father

A Few Famous Athlonians

Patrick J Lenihan who served as a TD; both Sean Fallon and Liam Naughton had very distinguished careers in the Seanad and happily there are Athlone members serving in both the Dail and Seanad at present.

In entertainment we have produced actors of note, musicians who hold (or have held) Irish championship titles, the distinguished tenor Louis Browne and the popular singer Brendan Shine. The great Irish bandmaster, Patrick Sarsfield Gilmore, learned his music in Athlone.

The authors Sax Rohmer (creator of the Fu Manchu novels), and James T Farrell (the author of the Mickey Spillane novels) had strong Athlone connections. There are several modern writers from Athlone whose work deserves mention: the poet Conleth Ellis who published several collections of poetry in both Irish and English; Sean O'Regan writer and publisher of Gandon Press; poet and publisher Desmond Egan of The Goldsmith Press; Sean O'Leochain, a distinguished poet in the Irish language; Joe Ducke, author and playwright and Breda Sullivan, a published poet.

Athlone has also produced many distinguished academics including Dr Patrick Murray, literary critic and historian; Dr Harman Murtagh, historian; Dr Anthony Kelly, mathematician; and several distinguished physicists including Fr Julian McCrea and Rev Dr Ciaran Ryan and Dr R.F. O'Connell.

What follows is, I hope, a representative selection of famous Athlonians. The task of compiling a more comprehensive biographical dictionary of famous Athlonians is for another time.

JOHN BRODERICK

The novelist John Broderick was born in Athlone in 1924, and died in Bath in 1989. He was educated St Peter's Infants' School and the Dean Kelly Memorial School. He spent further short periods in the Marist College, Athlone, and Summerhill College, before he enrolled in St Joseph's College, Garbally, Ballinasloe where he was to remain until 1941. John got an honours Intermediate Certificate but did not sit his Leaving Certificate. Instead he returned to the 'University of Life' where he combined the tasks of learning the skills of running a bakery with his determination to become a writer.

From the age of eighteen he was a compulsive writer. It was not until 1956 that the merits of his style and content were recognised when *The Irish Times* accepted a number of travel articles from him. Later when he was offered the opportunity to review books for that paper John Broderick had, perhaps, found his true vocation. As a book reviewer John had few equals – he was certainly in the first rank of Irish reviewers.

John Broderick's first book the *The Pilgrimage* was published in 1961 and The Censorship Board quickly banned it. In the United States it was published as *The Chameleons* it was also translated into French *Le Pelerinage.*

John Broderick went on to write a dozen novels four of which were translated into French. *An Apology for roses* was the most successful in terms of sales but stylistically *The Waking of Willie Ryan* was perhaps his most accomplished novel. The first John Broderick Weekend was held in Athlone in 1999 when the highlight was the dedication of a street to him. Athlone UDC became one of the first local authorities in Ireland to honour a twentieth century literary figure.

Apart from his novels he has been the subject of a biography. Madeline Kingston's *Something in the head: the life and work of John Broderick* which was published by The Lilliput Press in 2004 and an excellent volume of his selected writings *Stimulus of sin,* edited by Madeline Kingston and published by The Lilliput Press in 2007.

SEAN COSTELLO

Sean Costello was a native of Cornamagh, Athlone and was one of those who gave his young life for the cause of Ireland. He was educated at the local national school in Cornamaddy and after school worked for Peadar Melinn who had an egg-store beside the Royal Hotel.

About 1913 he left Athlone to get work in Dublin and there he became an 2nd Lieutenant with F Company, 1st Battalion of the Irish Volunteers. He was chosen to serve as a pall-bearer at the funeral of O'Donovan Rossa and obviously heard Padraig Pearse's oration at the grave-side in Glasnevin.

He took part in the Easter Rising and on the Wednesday of Easter Week, the bloodiest day of the Rebellion, when intense fighting was taking place at Mount Street Bridge an outpost of De Valera's command he was sent on despatch duty to Boland's Mill. In the aftermath of that encounter his body was found near Boland's Mill and he was buried in Glasnevin Cemetery. In 1935 Athlone UDC agreed to change the name of Irishtown to Sean Costello Street in his honour.

ARCHBISHOP MICHAEL J CURLEY

Michael J Curley was born in Golden Island in 1879. He was educated by the Marist Brothers before attending Mungret College, Limerick. He received his B.A. from the Royal University, Dublin and his S.T.L. from Rome. In March 1904 he was ordained in Rome.

His first mission took him to Florida where he became the first resident pastor of De Land. In 1905 he was appointed Chancellor of the diocese of St Augustine and at 34 years of age was appointed bishop. During the next seven years almost forty new churches were built in his diocese. He was a strong advocate of outlawing racial discrimination.

In 1921 he was appointed as Archbishop of Baltimore in succession to Cardinal Gibbons. In the following eighteen years he had established sixty-six new Catholic schools. In 1939 the See of Washington was added to Baltimore and he became the first archbishop to rule over two archdioceses simultaneously. He was a life-long friend of John Count McCormack. He died in 1947.

THOMAS FLINN V.C.

Thomas Flinn, who was born in Athlone in 1842 has the distinction of being one of two youngest ever Victoria Cross winners. Flinn who served as a drummer with the 64th regiment (North Staffordshire Regiment) won his V.C. at Cawnpore during the Indian Mutiny in 1857. He was aged just 15 years and three months at the time of the incident.

Drummer Flinn was involved in a charge on the enemy's guns on 28th November, 1857. Though he was injured himself he still engaged in a hand-to-hand combat with two rebel artillerymen. He killed both rebels and helped to capture the artillery piece. Both he and his commanding officer, Lt. Havelock, were awarded the Victoria Cross.

Within five years of his return to Athlone he was before the courts charged with stealing a pair of shoes belonging to an officer of his regiment. He served a month in prison for this offence. His later military career was undistinguished.

Thomas Flinn fell on hard times and when he sought admission to Athlone Workhouse he had to forfeit his V.C. pension to the Board of Guardians. He died in penury at the age of 50, his brave deeds apparently long forgotten. He was buried by the Guardians in a pauper's grave in Cornamagh cemetery. He is commemorated in the Garrison Church, Whittington Barracks, Lichfield, Staffordshire and the whereabouts of his medal is unknown.

EVELYN GLEESON

Evelyn Gleeson was born in Cheshire, to Irish parents, in 1855. She moved to Athlone as a child as her father, Dr Edward Moloney Gleeson, had founded of Athlone Woollen Mills a few years earlier.

She trained as a teacher but later decided to study art and design in London. She later spent six months under Alexander

Miller at South Kensington where she showed great skill and several of her designs were purchased by a leading Scottish carpet manufacturer.

In London she was associated with the Irish Literary Society, founded by W.B. Yeats and with the Gaelic League. She became friendly with the Yeats sisters, Elizabeth and Lily, sharing their interest in craft work and wanting to be part of the Irish revival.

Due to her ill-health, Dr Augustine Henry, an old family friend encouraged her to return to Ireland. It was with his capital and advice that she set up of Dun Emer Industries in her house in Dundrum in 1902. Here she supervised the hand-weaving of carpets, rugs and tapestries which she also designed. The emphasis was on Celtic ornament and in time the Yeats sisters joined her and undertook embroidery and printing under the Dun Emer Industries banner. The partnership broke down in 1908, Evelyn continued weaving as the Dun Emer Guild while the Miss Yeats set up the Cuala Industries in Churchtown, Co. Dublin.

In 1910 she became a founder member of the Guild of Irish Art Workers. She collaborated with her niece, Katherine MacCormack, for the design of the tapestries for the Honan Chapel, Cork. Evelyn Gleeson died in 1944 in her eighty-ninth year.

Hanna Greally

Johanna Greally was born in Athlone in 1925. Her family lived on the corner of Pearse Street and Connolly Street where Higgins Lounge is now. Neighbours remember her as a quiet girl but something happened at nineteen which resulted in her being admitted to a mental hospital. For over twenty years, always convinced of her sanity, Hanna Greally was an inmate in St Loman's Hospital, Mullingar.

She eventually negotiated her own release and chose to live near Roscommon where she devoted her life to writing and gardening.

Her book *Bird's Nest Soup* which is of course autobiographical became a best-seller. It was published in 1971. The book gives a gripping picture of life in a provincial asylum. Through the visits of her much loved mother she retained a link with normality and the hopes for eventual freedom. Despite the experiences it describes the book lacks bitterness it is full of humanity and compassion and truly a minor master-piece.

She died in 1987 and is buried in Cornamagh cemetery.

A Few Famous Athlonians

John Count McCormack

John McCormack was born in the Bawn in Athlone in 1884. He received his early education from the Marist Brothers in Athlone before attending Summerhill College, Sligo. As a boy he sang in the choir of St Peter's Church and was encouraged by the choirmaster Michael Kilkelly.

His career blossomed after he won the gold medal in the tenor section of the Dublin Feis Ceoil. He later studied in Italy under Sabatini. He made his operatic debut at Covent Gardens in 1907, and later turned his attention to the concert stage where he achieved worldwide success.

John McCormack went on to become one of leading tenors of his day and by today's standards a super-star. He had a very successful recording career and made two Hollywood films. He was rewarded for his work for Catholic charities by being made a Count of the Papal Court.

He died in Dublin in 1945. There is a bronze bust of John McCormack by Seamus Murphy on the Promenade in Athlone, and he has been the subject of a number of books. Anyone wishing to learn more about McCormack should read *The Great Irish tenor: John McCormack* by Gordon T. Ledbetter, published in Dublin by Town House in 2003.

T. P. O'Connor

Thomas Power O'Connor was born in Castle Street in 1848. His father was a 'billiard saloon keeper'. As a child he attended the Model School. He was brought home to attend the new diocesan College at Summerhill, Athlone. His mother later put him through college in Galway from where he graduated with a degree in History and Modern Languages in 1866.

In 1867 he was given a trial (without pay) with *Saunder's Newsletter*. He proved himself so useful that he was quickly employed. In 1870 he moved to London and worked for the *Daily Telegraph* and later in the Fleet Street offices of the *New York Herald*.

Having applied for a job as a publisher's reader he was interviewed by the publisher S. O. Beeton who proposed that T. P. should write a book himself. His first book was on Disraeli and he went on to produce another fifteen books on various topics.

He stood as an Irish Nationalist candidate in the General Election of 1880 and was returned as the Irish Nationalist MP for Galway. By 1885 he was the president of the Irish National League of Great Britain. The Irish in Liverpool invited him to contest a seat there and he became the MP for the 'Scotland division of Liverpool'.

In 1887 he founded his first newspaper *The Star*. He employed George Bernard Shaw as an assistant leader-writers and music critic. When he found himself in financial difficulties he sold *The Star* but with the help of the money received he founded *The Sunday Sun*. He later founded two more journals before he started *T. P.'s Weekly* in 1902. It ceased publication during the War but was revived in 1923 and lasted for a further six years until T. P. resigned because of ill health. He served as the first British film censor, a position he held until his death. At the time of his death in 1929 he was 'Father of the House of Commons' and a member of the Privy Council.

In 2005 Athlone Town Council named a street in his honour.

Harry Rice

Though born in Portarlington in 1894 Harry Rice was closely identified with Athlone. He was educated at Enniskillen and Trinity College where he qualified as a doctor. He served with the Royal Army Medical Corps during World War I and later as Port Embarkation Officer in Brussels.

Following his release from the British Army he joined the Indian Army where he served for a further twenty-five years. He had a close relationship with Athlone as two of his sisters had married Chapman brothers of Athlone Printing Works.

In 1922 he married his first wife, Lillian Geoghegan, a daughter of the proprietor of the Prince of Wales Hotel, Athlone. After her death in 1951 he married Cynthia MacWeeney. Harry Rice retired to Athlone and wrote a weekly column for *The Westmeath Independent*. He was a founder member of the Inland Waterway Association of Ireland and the author of a classic book on the Shannon *Thanks for the memory* originally published in 1952 and reprinted a number of times since.

Richard Rothwell

Richard Rothwell was born in Northgate Street, Athlone in 1800. He entered the Dublin's Society art school in 1814 and spent five years studying there. He was skilled at drawing and in 1820 won a silver medal. From early in his career he was determined to be a portrait painter.

In 1824 he was elected as an associate of the Royal Hibernian Academy and became a full member in 1826. He exhibited at the R.H.A. until 1829 when he moved to London. He quickly became an established portraitist and was commissioned by aristocrats and royalty.

In 1831 he moved to Italy for three years to study the Old Masters. On his return to London he found it difficult to re-establish himself and decided to diversify and paint history and subject paintings. He was restless in England and returned to

A Few Famous Athlonians

Dublin in 1847 but only stayed five years. He went back to London in 1852 and stayed there until he departed for America in 1854.

Rothwell remained unsettled and moved from America to London and from there to Rome. He failed to re-find that early promise and wandered aimlessly around Europe. He died in Rome in 1868. Had he managed to pursue his career as a portrait painter he would surely have been a major artist.

RICHARD & GRIZEL STEEVENS

One of the most famous vicars of Athlone in the 17th century was John Steevens. He had twin children, a son Richard and daughter Grizel. Richard was intended for the church but having matriculated c1670 he became a physician and in 1687 he graduated with a doctorate in medicine. In 1710 he was appointed regius professor of physic at Trinity College and president of the College of Physicians but died the same year. As one of the leading physicians of his day he accumulated great wealth which he left to his sister Grizel for her lifetime with the stipulation that after her death the remaining estate would be applied towards the foundation and maintenance of a hospital. Grizel Steevens devoted her energies to the fulfilment of her brother's wishes and opened 'Dr Steevens' Hospital' in Dublin during her own lifetime.

DR G.T. STOKES

One of the earliest professional historians to record the history of the Parish of Athlone was the Rev G.T. Stokes, a native of the town who was born in 1843. He studied at Galway Grammar School and at Queen's College, Galway before completing his studies at Trinity College Dublin.

A member of a prominent Church of Ireland family living in Tholsel Place (later Victoria Place and now Custume Place), George Thomas Stokes studied for the Church. He was ordained in 1866 and appointed as curate of St Patrick's parish, Newry the following year. In 1883 he was appointed to the chair of Ecclesiastical History at Trinity College.

In 1887 Dr Stokes was appointed Librarian of Marsh's Library, Dublin. In the same year he was elected to membership of the Royal Society of Antiquaries of Ireland. He was a frequent contributor to the prestigious journal of that society. Stokes wrote guides to Blackrock (Co. Dublin) and his native Athlone as well as major works on *Ireland and the Celtic Church* and *Ireland and the Anglo-Norman Church*. At the time of his death in 1898 he was engaged in presenting a major series of lectures on *Great Irish Churchmen of the 18th Century* and these were posthumously published in 1900 as *Some Worthies of the Irish Church*.

Bibliography

Beirne, Francis (ed), *The Diocese of Elphin: people, places and pilgrimage,* Dublin, The Columba Press, 2000

Burke, John, *Athlone in the Victorian era,* Athlone, Old Athlone Society, 2006

Cahill, Sean et al, *Lough Ree and its islands,* Athlone, Three Counties Press, 2006

Collins, Tom, *Athlone golf club 1892-1992,* Athlone, Athlone Golf Club, 1992

Delany, Ruth, *By Shannon shores,* Dublin, Gill and Macmillan, 1987

Egan, Frank, *Athlone's golden mile,* Athlone, the author, 1980

English, N.W., *Lough Ree Yacht Club 1770-1970: a memoir*, Athlone, LRYC, 1970

Fallon, Rosaleen & Michael (ed), *Clonown: the history, traditions and culture of a South Roscommon community,* Athlone, Clonown Community Centre, 1989

Heery, Stephen, *The Shannon floodlands: a natural history*, Galway, Tir Eolas, 1983

Keaney, Marian & Gearoid O'Brien, *Athlone bridging the centuries*, Mullingar, Westmeath County Council, 1991

Lenehan, Jim, *Politics and society in Athlone 1830-1885: a rotten Borough,* Dublin, Irish Academic Press, 1999

Murtagh, Harman, *Athlone: history and settlement to 1800*, Athlone, Old Athlone Society, 2000

Murtagh, Harman, *No 6, Athlone. Historic Towns Atlas*, Dublin, Royal Irish Academy, 1996

Murtagh, Harman (ed), *Irish midland studies: essays in commemoration of N.W. English*, Athlone, Old Athlone Society, 1980

Murtagh, Harman & Michael O'Dwyer (ed), *Athlone besieged: eyewitness and other contemporary accounts of the sieges of Athlone, 1690 and 1691,* Athlone, Temple Printing Co and Old Athlone Society, 1991

O'Brien, Brendan, *Athlone Workhouse and the Famine,* Athlone, Old Athlone Society, 1995

O'Brien, Gearoid, 'Athlone Miscellany' in *The Westmeath Independent,* 1990-2008

O'Brien, Gearoid (ed), *Athlone tourist trail*, Athlone, Athlone Chamber of Commerce, 2nd ed., 1991

O'Brien, Gearoid, *The Lough Ree trail*, Mullingar, Westmeath Tourism Council, 1990

O'Brien, Gearoid, *St Mary's parish, Athlone: a history*, Longford, St. Mel's Diocesan Trust, 1989

Piers, Sir Henry, *A Chorographical description of the county of Westmeath*, Tara, Meath Archaeological and Historical Society, 1981

Praeger, Robert L, *The Way that I went,* Dublin, Hodges, Figgis & Co., 1939

Ryan, Hazel, *Athlone Abbey graveyard inscriptions*, Mullingar, Longford Westmeath Joint Library Committee, 1987

Dear Reader
This book is from our much complimented illustrated book series which includes:-

Belfast	Blanchardstown, Castleknock and the Park
By the Lough's North Shore	Dundrum, Stillorgan & Rathfarnham
East Belfast	Blackrock, Dun Laoghaire and Dalkey
South Belfast	Bray and North Wicklow
Antrim, Town & Country	Dublin 4
North Antrim	Limerick's Glory
Across the Roe	Galway on the Bay
Inishowen	Connemara
Donegal Highlands	The Book of Clare
Donegal, South of the Gap	Kildare
Donegal Islands	Carlow
Islands of Connaught	Monaghan
Sligo	Athlone
Mayo	Cavan
North Kerry	Kilkenny
Fermanagh	Armagh
Omagh	Ring of Gullion
Cookstown	Carlingford Lough
Dundalk & North Louth	The Mournes
Drogheda & the Boyne Valley	Heart of Down
Fingal	Strangford's Shores
Dublin's North Coast	Lecale

Cottage Publications
is an imprint of
Laurel Cottage Ltd
15 Ballyhay Road
Donaghadee, Co. Down
N. Ireland, BT21 0NG

We can also supply prints, individually signed by the artist, of the paintings featured in many of the above titles as well as many other areas of Ireland.

For details on these superb publications and to view samples of the paintings they contain, you can visit our web site
www.cottage-publications.com
or alternatively you can contact us as follows:–
Telephone: +44 (0)28 9188 8033
Fax: +44 (0)28 9188 8063

For the more athletically minded our illustrated walking book series includes:–

Bernard Davey's Mourne	**Tony McAuley's Glens**
Rathlin, An Island Odyssey	**Bernard Davey's Mourne Part 2**

We also have an exciting new range which cover rivers in Ireland and includes:–

By the Banks of the Bann	**The Liffey**
My Lagan Love	**Following the Foyle**